From
Paragraph
to Theme

Herman Hudson
Maurice Imhoof
Indiana University

MACMILLAN PUBLISHING CO., INC.
New York

From Paragraph to Theme

Understanding and Practice

Macmillan Publishing Co., Inc.
866 Third Avenue, New York, New York 10022

Collier-Macmillan Canada, Ltd.

Printing: 2 3 4 5 6 7 8 9   Year: 4 5 6 7 8 9

Preface

If the thought structures and relationships in paragraphs are weak, the larger essay or theme will almost invariably lack order, clarity, and conviction. This book treats the structure of the paragraph and provides a repertoire of different techniques of paragraph organization that a writer may eventually select from and use effectually.

Each lesson consists of one or more model paragraphs followed by exercises analyzing the characteristics of the models to develop a general understanding of their form. Every third lesson in the book unites the techniques presented in preceding chapters, requiring analysis and construction of a theme or long paper. The final lesson is devoted wholly to the theme, requiring writing skills practiced throughout the text.

Above all, the book is concerned with the college composition, for that is still a tangible measure of standard competence and education in most instances. The models exemplify, in some cases, typical writing assignments or textbook styles in history, psychology, sociology, and other subjects. Other examples present material on blacks, Puerto Ricans, and Mexican Americans, and on rock music, film criticism, urban economics, and Afro-American studies. These selections demonstrate the immediacy of composition to all of the curriculum and help balance the more formal, academic uses of composition with its application to *people* and *ideas* that are both neglected and urgent as subjects for serious writing.

Some techniques of paragraph development can be learned easily if they are demonstrated clearly and practiced carefully. The understanding and practice of these techniques should enable the student to write simply and clearly on topics that he has previously thought about. He will also be encouraged to study consciously the ways in which other writers express and organize their ideas.

Many of the model paragraphs and exercises have been tested at Indiana University in a special program in which high school graduates from our urban areas are given a summer's work on campus before entry into the regular academic program. Since 1969, the program has brought some 200 students to campus each summer. The groups have included blacks, Mexican Americans, Puerto Ricans, Appalachian whites, and others, chiefly students who have had previous *instruction* but limited *success* in writing. The method of the text has been productive with these students because it does not get bogged down in the detailed sentence-level errors of grammar, usage, and punctuation. Instead, it gives attention to the larger organizational devices, making it easier to treat the sentence-level errors (for which other instructional materials are available) in their proper relationship to overall writing skills. The method does not penalize students for "weak content" or "lack of ideas" or for having "nothing to say." Rather, it provides, through model paragraphs, content relevant to the students and asks them to write on subjects about which they do have something to say.

H. H.
M. I.

Contents

Introduction   1

1 Paragraph Development by Listing   5

2 Paragraph Development by Examples   15

3 Theme Development by Examples   23

4 Paragraph Development by Comparison   31

5 Paragraph Development by Contrast   43

6 Theme Development by Comparison and Contrast   57

7 Paragraph Development by Definition   65

8 Paragraph Development by Classification   87

9 Theme Development by Definition and Classification   99

10 Paragraph Development by Space and Time   107

11 Paragraph Development by Process Description   131

12 Theme Development by Time, Space, and Process   149

13 Paragraph Development by Cause and Effect   159

14 Paragraph Development by Generalization   171

15 Theme Development by Various Means   183

From Paragraph to Theme

Introduction

People have lost reverence for the printed page and have gained an independence from it through the increasing availability of such nonprint media as recordings, cassettes, films, and television. In spite of the many magazines and newspapers that have failed— because of television, they say—reading is still very much a key to your success in acquiring the information and knowledge essential to formal education, and writing is still the primary tool for recording and organizing your knowledge into useful and reusable notes. Writing is also the primary medium of communication to demonstrate to your instructors that you have acquired the information and skills necessary to join the ranks of the educated. In the general world of work and pleasure, you may not be asked to do much formal "writing," but you will be surrounded and sometimes victimized by other people's writing all your life. In both high school and college the art of writing (or composition as it is traditionally called) is one chance for academic success you have a great deal of control over. You should take the opportunity to master it now.

The purpose of this textbook is to help you gain

confidence and skill in writing college compositions. A *composition* is any organized, self-contained piece of writing written—or "composed"—for a special purpose, often an assignment in class. The term is frequently used for writing assignments in an English or composition class, where it usually means a self-conscious process in which you may make thoughtful decisions concerning what to say first, how to organize and develop your ideas, and what words to use.

Writing good compositions requires the mastery of several skills. It requires grammatical accuracy and acceptability so that relationships between words are clear and understanding between reader and writer is made easier. It requires that the mechanics of punctuation, capitalization, spelling, footnoting, perhaps even handwriting follow acceptable conventions. Additionally, it requires vocabulary appropriate to the subject matter and the level and tone of writing. Finally, writing a good composition requires a careful and planned structuring of ideas. It is this skill—the structuring of ideas—which receives attention in this book. The book is not intended to teach you everything you need to know to be a better writer, and should provide only a part of your resources for writing improvement.

Although personal feelings and self-expression in writing may be rewarded in some classes, most instructors require demonstration that you know the facts. Your understanding of these facts and information about your subject are most commonly presented through educated prose—structured, disciplined, thoughtful composition. We feel we can best show how ideas are structured through direct attention to the techniques of development used in writing paragraphs. This book therefore focuses on the organizational foundation of all expository writing, the paragraph. Themes, or longer compositions, are treated as extensions of the techniques shown in writing paragraphs about people, events, and ideas.

Let us explain next how we hope to accomplish our aim of enabling you to write better paragraphs. Specifically, each lesson in the text gives you a number of model paragraphs to read and study. The paragraphs in one lesson demonstrate or exemplify one technique of paragraph development. Exercises that closely follow the organization of the model paragraphs provide you with an *analysis* of the particular paragraph's structure as a basis for a general *understanding* of paragraph development. This general understanding is then employed in additional exercises and homework assignments that require *practice* of the writing techniques demonstrated in the lesson. The lessons foster a sense of progress, because mastery of a specific technique or skill is achieved in each lesson before the next one is undertaken. Every third lesson in the text extends the techniques learned to a theme or long paper.

It may appear in individual lessons that we encourage practice of a particular type of paragraph development for its own sake. This is not the case. We have tried to select only a few of the most useful types of paragraph organization, but they are useful only in that they satisfy the organizational requirements of your particular writing task. The writing practice is intended to build up a repertoire of several different types of paragraph development which, with increasing ease, you can select from and use effectively in your own writing assignments. In Chapter 15 and elsewhere, we show that these are not simply methods of development we made up, but those that appear with frequency in the formal writings of others. The ultimate goal we see for you is the ability to approach any subject with the confidence that you can develop and express your ideas on that subject through the methods discussed in this text.

The general subject matter of this book is, of course, writing—a subject about which you may or may not share our enthusiasm. In either case, we have tried to make the particular subject matter of the model paragraphs reflect matters of interest and experiences of general concern. Some topics for model paragraphs were chosen because they are typical of the writing assignments in history, psychology, sociology, and so on. Other topics were chosen because they help demonstrate the techniques of development we feel are most productive. But all were chosen because we consider them legitimate classroom topics frequently ignored in traditional composition texts. We have deliberately included material on blacks, Puerto Ricans, Mexican Americans, on rock music, film criticism, urban economics, and Black Studies. Demonstrating that neglected *people* and *ideas* are as appropriate as subjects for writing as the more conventional "academic" topics is a major goal of this book.

We believe there are a few techniques of paragraph development that can be learned easily if they are clearly demonstrated and carefully practiced. The understanding and practice of these techniques should have the immediate result of enabling you to write simply and clearly about a variety of topics on which you already have ideas. It should also encourage you to continue the conscious study of the ways in which ideas are organized and expressed in the writings of others as well as in your own. We further believe that the mastery of these techniques will assure success in this course and most certainly increase the prospect of success in any course requiring a substantial amount of writing.

Paragraph Development by Listing

1.1 Read the model paragraph. As you read, pay close attention to both the meaning and the organization of the ideas discussed.

Sentence Functions in Paragraph Development

The sentences of most well-written paragraphs may be analyzed into four general functions. First, there are paragraph intoducers, which are sentences that establish the topic focus of the paragraph as a whole. Second, there are paragraph developers, which present examples or details of various kinds that support the ideas set forth by the paragraph introducers. Third, there are viewpoint or context modulators, which are sentences that provide a smooth transition between different sets of ideas. Fourth, there are paragraph terminators, which logically bring the ideas discussed in the paragraph to a psychologically satisfying conclusion. Not all paragraphs will be composed of these four sentence types; however, most successful ones will contain a combination of some of them.

1.1a According to the information given, what is the

purpose of a paragraph introducer? Does the first sentence of the
model paragraph function as a paragraph introducer?

1.1b What function do paragraph developers serve? Identify the
paragraph developers used in the model paragraph.

1.1c Is the final sentence in the model paragraph a good
terminator? That is, does it round off the paragraph by bringing it
to a satisfying conclusion?

1.1d The type of paragraph presented above is called a *list
paragraph.* To avoid a "shopping list" appearance, certain words or
phrases are used to help the paragraph proceed smoothly. Point
out the words or devices that are employed to aid the listing of
details.

1.2 Read the model paragraph. This time as you read try to
observe three main parts of paragraph organization.

Black Personalities in Public Life

The decade of the 1960's brought an upsurge in the number of
blacks appointed or elected to important offices throughout the
country. In 1967, for example, Thurgood Marshall, a graduate of
Howard University Law School, was appointed the first black
Associate Justice of the U.S. Supreme Court. In the 1968 national
elections, Shirley Chisholm won a seat in the Brooklyn 12th
Congressional District to become the first black woman in
Congress. On Capitol Hill in Washington, D.C., is Senator Edward
Brooke of Massachusetts. Another new political figure is Julian
Bond, representative in the Georgia State Legislature, who won
national attention by being nominated for the vice-presidency at
the Democratic Convention in Chicago. Two other leaders prominent in municipal government are Richard Hatcher of Gary and
Carl Stokes of Cleveland, the first elected black mayors of large
U.S. cities. While those mentioned thus far are currently active in
public life, the two men who have undoubtedly had the most
decisive impact on black people in the second half of the twentieth
century are no longer living. Malcolm X, assassinated leader of the
Black Muslims, advocated militant action as the only solution to
racial inequities. Martin Luther King, Jr., slain head of the
Southern Christian Leadership Conference, typified the nonviolent

approach in the acquisition of civil rights. This brief and incomplete list of black leaders symbolizes the increasing participation of black people in the affairs of the nation.

1.2a Does this paragraph contain the essential elements of a well-written paragraph—introducer, developers, terminator? Point out the sentence or sentences that serve as the introducer, the developers, the terminator.

1.2b In addition to the three types of sentences mentioned in the previous question, this paragraph contains a viewpoint or context modulator, that is, a transition sentence. Remember that this is a sentence that provides a transition between different sets of ideas. Identify the sentence that performs this transition function. What two sets of ideas does it connect?

1.2c In the model paragraph of 1.1, transitional words such as *first* and *second* are used in the development of the paragraph. In the model paragraph of 1.2, other words—*for example, another,* etc.—are used for the same purpose. Find these words in the paragraph. For each, explain how it relates one idea to another.

1.2d Review (see sentence 5 of paragraph 1.1 and exercise 1.1c) the function of a paragraph terminator. Is the final sentence of 1.2 an adequate terminator?

1.3 The following list paragraph gives information about several black women singers. How many of these artists are familiar to you?

They Also Sing the Classics

Most younger Americans are familiar with the brilliant recordings and performances of such singers as Dionne Warwick, Aretha Franklin, and Diana Ross, but neither the patrons of pop music nor the general American public is aware that numerous talented black women have also achieved distinction in the field of classical music. Felicia Weathers is a talented soprano of the rising younger generation of stars. Contralto Grace Bumbry made her debut with the Metropolitan Opera in 1965, as Princess Eboli in "Don Carlo." Shirley Verrett, a mezzo-soprano, has sung with leading symphony orchestras throughout the country. Leontyne Price is the gifted

Metropolitan Opera soprano for whom Samuel Barber, a contemporary American composer, wrote the cycle "The Hermit Songs."
Soprano Dorothy Maynor had an outstanding singing career before
she became the founder and director in 1963 of the Harlem School
of the Arts and a member of the Board of Directors of
Westminster Choir College. Singer-performer Marian Anderson,
perhaps the most famous of all black singers during the 1940's and
1950's, has left a rich catalogue of recordings including a collection
of her favorite art songs for studio study.

1.3a Does the paragraph meet the requirements of a list paragraph?
1.3b Identify the paragraph developers. Note that no connectors
—transitional words or phrases—are employed. Reread the paragraph, inserting at the beginning of sentences 2 through 6 the
transitional words, in order, that follow:

for example   one other famous black singer
also   finally
another

1.3c Notice that no terminator sentence is used. Choose a
terminator sentence from the following three sentences and justify
your choice:

1. Many black men are also famous singers.
2. These women are a few of the black singers who have
   achieved success in classical music.
3. Perhaps the reason that some of these names are so
   unfamiliar is that most Americans don't listen to classical
   music.

1.4 Most Americans are enthusiastically interested in sports of all
kinds. The typical sports fan is generally eager to share his
enthusiasm and his knowledge of sports events and personalities
with the uninitiated. If you wanted to write about a certain aspect
of the 1968 Olympic games, would the following paragraph serve
as one possible model for organizing and presenting your ideas?

Black Athletes at the 1968 Olympics

Despite rarefied air and threatened boycotts, black members of the 1968 U.S. Olympic team led the country to unprecedented victories in Mexico City. Bob Beamon, for instance, established a world's record with his long jump of 29'2½". Another international record went to Tommy Smith with a 200-meter sprint of 19.8 seconds. In the 100-meter category, Jimmy Hines earned a gold medal for his 9.9-second dash. His female counterpart, Wyomia Tyus, set a world's record in the women's 100-meter dash. Lee Evans, also a sprinter, was awarded a gold medal for his 43.8-second time in the 400-meter competition. In another sport, heavyweight boxer George Foreman collected a gold medal for his

performance. _____

_____

_____

_____

_____

_____

These eight athletes are a few of the many blacks who helped amass 45 gold medals won by the U.S. team.

1.4a What is the name and function of the first sentence in the model paragraph of 1.4?

1.4b What is the name and function of sentences 2 through 7 in the paragraph?

1.4c What is the name and function of the final sentence?

1.4d List the transitional words or phrases. Explain how they connect the different sentences.

1.4e Name two other black athletes who performed in the 1968 Olympics and list them within the body of paragraph 1.4. Remember to use connecting words.

1.5 As you read the next paragraph, try to make an objective evaluation of yourself in relation to the points mentioned.

As the new decade of the 1970's begins, one wonders what personal qualities will be required for success. Possibly the three most essential attributes are flexibility, sensitivity, and honesty. First, our rapidly changing society necessitates flexibility—the ability to adapt oneself readily to new ideas and experiences. Next, a person must cultivate his sensitivity; he must be aware of and understand the needs of others. Finally, honesty, the capacity for "telling it like it is," will be important in all aspects of personal and public relations. Although these attributes are desirable today, in the future they will become even more decisive in determining personal success.

1.5a Although this is also a list paragraph, it differs slightly in form from the previous ones. Notice that there are two sentences that function as paragraph introducers. The first is a topic introducer, which establishes the topic of discussion. The second sentence, the topic sentence, more narrowly defines—or delimits—the topic. In this case, we know that the discussion will be limited to three attributes. Discuss with your classmates and teacher other personal qualities that you believe are important for success. If one or two of these were to become a part of the body of the paragraph, how would you rewrite the topic sentence? For example, if you add *creativity* and *perseverance* to the list, you must make all necessary changes in the topic sentence to account for the new elements. Write the new topic sentence in the following blanks.

1.5b What connectors, or transitional words, were used in the original paragraph?

1.5c Write a title in the blank space provided directly above the paragraph. Look at the titles of other paragraphs in the lesson. Notice that a good title is brief and gives some indication of the content or point of view of the paragraph. The topic introducer and the topic sentence provide the necessary information for you to write a good title.

1.5d Discuss with your teacher and fellow students the concepts of flexibility, sensitivity, and honesty. Name some famous people or personal acquaintances who possess these qualities.

1.6 Remember that a list paragraph has several parts. First, paragraph introducers—both a topic introducer and a topic sentence or just a topic sentence—are used to open a paragraph. Next, supporting examples are listed with the aid of connectors. Transition or modulator sentences are used between different sets of ideas. Finally, a terminator sentence brings the paragraph to a logical conclusion.

With these ideas in mind, write your own list paragraph. Give your paragraph a title. You may choose one of the topics given below.

Contemporary black writers
Popular soul groups
Qualities of a good teacher (or leader or friend)
Black athletes at the 1972 Olympics
Topic of your choice

1.6(a)   Name _____ **Date** _____

_____

_____

_____

_____

_____

_____

_____

_____

_____

_____

_____

_____

_____

_____

_____

_____

_____

_____

_____

Paragraph Development by Examples

2.1 This lesson is concerned with the use of examples in the development of paragraphs. A kind of list paragraph, the body of the example paragraph consists of example sentences that closely support the topic sentence. There is, of course, a terminator. Examine the following paragraph:

Effective Writing—A Must in College

The ability to write well-organized, concise paragraphs is essential to a student's success in almost all college courses. For example, in reporting the results of a scientific experiment, a student must present his findings in logical order and appropriate language in order to receive a favorable evaluation of his work. To write successful answers to essay questions on history or anthropology examinations, a student must arrange the relevant facts and opinions according to some accepted pattern of paragraph structure. And certainly when a student writes a book report for English, or a critique for political science, or a term paper for sociology, style and organization are often as important as content. Clearly, skill in expository writing is crucial to successful achievement in most college subjects.

2.1a Familiarize yourself with the following symbols and defini-
tions that will be used in analyzing paragraph structure:

TS—stands for topic sentence, a sentence that states the main
idea of a paragraph.

E—stands for example sentence, a sentence that presents a
specific example or illustration related to the topic sentence.

R—stands for restatement sentence, a sentence that in essence
repeats or restates the main idea of the topic sentence in
different words. The restatement sentence gives the effect of
rounding off the paragraph by circling back to the idea of the
topic sentence. The restatement is one kind of paragraph
terminator.

2.1b Which sentence in the model paragraph of 2.1 expresses the
main idea of the paragraph? Remember that the sentence that
expresses the main idea of a paragraph is called the topic sentence
(TS).

2.1c What is the relationship between sentence 2 and sentence 1?
Which sentence expresses a general idea? Which sentence presents a
specific example (E)?

2.1d What is the relationship between sentence 3 and sentence 1?
What is the relationship between sentence 3 and sentence 2?

2.1e Does the final sentence function as an adequate terminator?
Why?

2.1f What symbols would you use to describe the structure of the

paragraph? _____

2.2 The sentences listed below are *not* arranged in the logical
paragraph sequence of topic sentence, examples, and restatement.
Study the list carefully and try to decide which sentence makes a
general statement, which sentences present illustrations, and which
sentence repeats the idea of the general statement. Write a number
before each sentence to show its logical position in a well-ordered
paragraph.

_5_   These and dozens of other corporations have indicated that
in the future they are willing to hire any black who is willing
to prepare.

E¹ 2   For example, Xerox has already adopted an employee recruitment policy that invites blacks to join the company in such fields as fundamental and applied research, engineering, manufacturing, computer programming, administration, and marketing.

E³ 4   Atlantic Richfield, a petroleum and energy company, is also seeking black personnel for positions in oil drilling, air-pollution control, and production of electricity from the atom.

T⁰ i   In the 1970's, black college graduates will have unlimited career opportunities in business and industry.

E² 3   General Foods, General Electric, American Telephone and Telegraph, First National City Bank of New York, and the Ford Motor Company all have established open-ended professional and executive training programs for promising black college graduates.

2.2a Discuss with your teacher and your classmates your reasons for arranging the sentences in the sequence you determined. Give reasons for arranging the developers in the sequence you used.

2.2b Read the sentences in the arrangement you have established in order to experience the paragraph as a unified whole.

2.2c What symbols would you use to describe the paragraph

structure? _____

2.3 Read the following paragraph, which contains four unfinished sentences. Complete the sentences by writing in appropriate song titles. Write only one title in each blank. Remember that the first word and all important words in a title should be capitalized.

_____

The lyrics of many popular songs represent a realistic treatment

of the gut issues of the day. The words of songs like _____

_____

and_____

express the determination of black people to achieve equal rights in a just American society. The struggle to overcome the frustration and poverty of ghetto life is illustrated in such songs as

_____

and _____ .

There are songs like _____

and _____ that deal with the search for dignity and respect in the love relationship between a man and a woman. And finally, the basic need of everyone to develop and express his individuality is

depicted in the words of _____ ,

_____ ,

and _____ . Far from being mere frivolous rhymes about the moon in June, many popular songs represent a serious attempt to portray the real problems of human existence.

2.3a What symbols would you use to describe the structure of

this paragraph? _____
2.3b Discuss in class the meanings of *gut issues, determination, frustration, individuality, frivolous.*
2.3c Write a title in the blank space provided directly above the paragraph.

2.4 As you read the partial paragraph that follows, think about what the generation gap means to you.

The Generation Gap

From clothing to ethics, every aspect of American life today seems dominated by the generation gap—the division alleged to exist between the young and anyone over thirty. In music, the fans of the big band era of Glenn Miller and Benny Goodman find the sounds of the Beatles or the hard rock of the Rolling Stones unnerving. Another instance of the difference in values involves education, where the acquisition of knowledge for its own sake is being challenged by a demand for relevance. Perhaps the most controversial aspect of the generation gap arises from conflicting

attitudes toward sex and the use of drugs. _____

_____

_____

_____

_____

_____

_____

_____

_____

_____

2.4a In part of the space provided above, add two more examples of your own of the generation gap.

2.4b Provide a terminator beginning with the words, "In conclusion," which will logically close the paragraph.

2.4c Using symbols, what is the structure of the resulting

paragraph? _____

2.4d Be prepared to define and explain the words *unnerving, acquisition, relevance, controversial.*

2.5 As you read the next paragraph, observe the transitional devises used to move from one example to another.

The Peace Corps

The Peace Corps, the volunteer service organization founded under the administration of John F. Kennedy, serves diverse purposes in the countries in which it operates. For instance, one function that Peace Corps Volunteers perform is to educate both native pupils and teachers. Another important service is to advise and assist agricultural development programs. Still other activities aid business and industry, transportation, and various construction projects such as dams, hospitals, schools, and homes. But perhaps the most valuable assistance offered is in the allied fields of public health, sanitation, nursing, and medicine. These examples briefly illustrate the wide-ranging objectives of the Peace Corps.

2.5a What symbols would you use to describe the structure of the

paragraph? _____
2.5b What words or devices are used for transitional purposes?
2.5c What do you know about VISTA volunteers? What do the letters in "VISTA" stand for?

2.6 Write an original paragraph on any subject illustrating the use of examples in the development of logical paragraph structure. Give your paragraph a title. You may choose one of the topics given below.

The VISTA volunteer program
Favorite TV programs
Telling it like it is
Topic of your choice

Theme Development by Examples

3

3.1 Read the model paragraph.

Black Performers and the Television Industry

The American television industry, which throughout most of its history restricted black performers to occasional guest appearances, since the beginning of the 1970's has begun to provide a variety of opportunities for talented blacks. For instance, the national networks and many local stations have opened up the field of news reporting and commentary to an increasing number of black reporters. Nonexistent a decade ago, appearances of black actors in all kinds of spot commercials are commonplace today. Even the "soap operas" have integrated; black actors regularly play nonstereotyped roles in so-called real-life situations. Perhaps the most convincing evidence of a change in policy is the fact that a few black performers now have starring roles in their own weekly TV shows. These and similar examples indicate a start toward the democratization of the television industry.

3.1a Using the symbols that were introduced in lesson two (2.1a) to describe the functional relationship of sentences in a paragraph, assign an appropriate symbol to each sentence in this paragraph.

Sentence 1 ____	Sentence 4 ____
Sentence 2 ____	Sentence 5 ____
Sentence 3 ____	Sentence 6 ____

3.1b What is the function of sentence 1? What role does it play in the paragraph?

3.1c What contribution to the development of the paragraph do sentences 2, 3, 4, and 5 make?

3.1d Is sentence 6 necessary to the structure of a well-written paragraph? If so, why? If not, why not?

3.1e Discuss in class the meanings of *stereotype, stereotyped, nonstereotyped, commentary, democratization, real-life situations.*

3.2 In the previous exercise (3.1a) the symbols that describe the organization of the model paragraph were indicated.

TS / E1, E2, E3, E4 / R

The plan of the paragraph is very simple; it consists of only three parts:

1. A topic sentence that presents a one-sentence statement of the main idea of the whole paragraph
2. Several example sentences that give details to support the main idea of the topic sentence
3. A restatement sentence that reaffirms the central idea of the topic sentence

The basic TS / E ... / R paragraph plan can be extended to provide the plan for a theme also consisting of three parts:

1. A topic paragraph (TP) that introduces the main idea of the whole theme
2. One or more example paragraphs (EP), each one of which presents a main point with its supporting details
3. A restatement paragraph (RP) that once again focuses attention on the main idea of the topic paragraph

As you read the following theme, try to observe its plan of organization.

Black Performers and the Television Industry

——   The television industry since the beginning of the 1970's has begun to provide a variety of opportunities for talented blacks. Throughout most of its history in America, television restricted black performers to guest appearances in song-and-dance routines in the minstrel-show tradition. Black celebrities sang or danced their way through an occasional brief spot on popular variety programs. In recent times, however, the industry has opened a number of different fields to black performers.

——   The national networks and many local stations utilize an increasing number of black reporters in the field of news reporting and commentary. To report on both the black and white communities, Chuck Stone, George Foster, Lem Tucker, and Bill Matney have been selected by network news departments. In New York, Detroit, Indianapolis, Cincinnati, and many other cities, local television stations employ black newsmen to write about and report or comment on local scenes and situations.

——   In the "dollars-and-cents" field of the industry, alleged sponsor fear of falling sales for their products previously prevented blacks from appearing in TV commercials. It is apparent that the fear was unfounded, and now in TV commercials blacks as well as whites drink instant coffee and use that margarine that tastes like butter. They make their windows sparkle with the right kind of window cleaner, wash their clothes in low-suds detergents, shower with deodorant soap, and prevent cavities with fluoride toothpaste. They drive cars and borrow money from the local bank. Nonexistent a decade ago, appearances of black actors playing "prestige" roles in all kinds of spot commercials are commonplace today.

——   Even the daily serials, the "soap operas," have integrated black actors in so-called real-life situations. Marriage, health, money, youth, problem areas common to black and white alike, provide the subjects on which the soap operas dwell. On such programs as "The Doctors" and "One Life to Live," blacks have appeared in roles that do not attempt to depict the special problems of being black, but instead try to portray black people in the routine problems of daily life in America.

____ In a few exceptional cases, a small number of black performers have had starring roles on weekly TV shows. Bill Cosby and Diahann Carroll both have depicted the central roles in their own successful comedy programs. Lloyd Haynes has starred as a school teacher in "Room 222." Flip Wilson has hosted a weekly variety show. Other black actors have appeared as regular members of the casts of "Mission Impossible" (Greg Morris), "Mod Squad" (Clarence Williams III), "Ironside" (Don Mitchell), "Mannix" (Gail Fisher). The use of black performers in key roles in regular series is perhaps the most convincing evidence of a changing policy by the television industry.

____ As they did in the past, black performers still appear as guests on regular and special variety shows, from the weekly Ed Sullivan Show to the annual Academy Awards presentations. More significantly, professional black performers are now filling roles once exclusively reserved for white actors. Talented blacks report the news, sell popular products through commercial messages, and act out the lives of both villains and heroes on the daily and weekly comedies and dramas. These and similar examples indicate a start toward the democratization of the television industry.

3.2a Label each paragraph in the model theme using the symbols TP (for topic paragraph), EP (for example paragraph), and RP (for restatement paragraph). Since there are several EP's, number them consecutively EP1, EP2, EP3, and so on.

3.2b Underline the topic sentence in the TP. Does this sentence also state the main idea of the whole theme?

3.2c Underline the sentence that states the main point in EP1. Does the main point of this paragraph come first in the paragraph?

3.2d What relationship do the unmarked sentences in EP1 have to the underlined sentence?

3.2e Underline the sentence that states the main point in EP2, in EP3, and in EP4. Do the main points of these paragraphs come first?

3.2f What relationship do the unmarked sentences in each example paragraph have to the underlined sentence in that paragraph?

3.2g Underline the restatement sentence in the RP. Does it come first in the paragraph? What relationship does it have to the unmarked sentences in this paragraph? Does the restatement sentence also round off the whole theme by referring back to the topic paragraph? If so, how?

3.2h Transitional words or phrases are important in writing a theme. They help connect and show the relationship of the various parts, or paragraphs, of the theme.

Study the following section on the various transitional devices used in the theme; notice how the transitional words or phrases move the reader from one topic to another, from one point of view to another, or from one example to another.

Paragraph	Transition	Relationship
TP	In recent times . . .	This changes the point of view from the history of American television to the beginning of the 1970's. The rest of the theme is about recent times.
TP	. . . a number of different fields . . .	Changes the topic from variety or song-and-dance programs to "a number of different fields." The example paragraphs that follow list these fields.
EP1	. . . in the field of news . . .	This relates the first example paragraph to the main topic in the TP—". . . the television industry has opened a number of different fields to black performers."
EP2	In the "dollars-and-cents" field of the industry . . .	This relates the second example paragraph to the main topic in the TP.
EP3	Even the daily serials, the "soap operas" . . .	The major transitional device is *even* and indicates a new example will be discussed. Notice that the world *field* is not needed in this paragraph. The name of the field is given—daily serials—but it is not necessary to repeat "in the field of . . . "

Paragraph	Transition	Relationship
EP4	In a few exceptional cases . . . weekly TV shows.	This indicates that still another example is coming. It is not as direct as the other transitions; but the words *weekly TV shows* indicate the name of the new field.
RP	As they did in the past . . .	This leads the reader back to the first paragraph where the history of TV was discussed.
RP	More significantly . . . now . . .	This moves the reader from the past, which is not so important in this theme, to something more important that is taking place now.

3.2i Now read the model paragraph 3.1 again to discover the relationship between the paragraph and the theme. Notice in the theme that the sentences you have underlined are exactly like, or nearly like, the sentences in the model paragraph. The TS in the model paragraph has been expanded to become the TP in the theme. E1 becomes the topic sentence for EP1. E2 becomes the topic sentence for EP2, and so on. The R in the model paragraph, of course, becomes the topic sentence in the RP.

3.3 The symbolic representation of the paragraph you are about to read is as follows: TS / E1, E2, E3 / R. As you read the paragraph, try to think of ways the various sentences could be expanded into separate paragraphs to form a theme.

Each year the American automotive industry produces a glittering array of cars designed to appeal to every age, to every taste, to every pocketbook. For the young, who demand the ultimate in appearance and performance, there is a great variety of sports and specialty models. For the "young at heart"—the over-forty solid citizen who wants a prestige mix of style, size, and comfort—there is a wide selection of big, sleek cars available with all sorts of optional equipment. And finally, for the really big spender, there is a select group of luxury cars, custom-built to the most fastidious taste. Truly, it can be said that the automobile industry exemplifies the seller's slogan, "You pay your money, and you take your choice."

3.3a   Give the paragraph a title.
3.3b   Using the procedures illustrated in 3.1 and 3.2, expand the five sentences of this paragraph into a theme of five paragraphs with the structure TP / EP1, EP2, EP3 / RP. Give the theme a title.

Paragraph Development by Comparison

4

4.1 A comparison paragraph, as its name indicates, compares similar aspects or qualities of two subjects. In this lesson two procedures will be followed. The first procedure in writing a comparison paragraph alternates an example related to one subject—A—with an example related to a second subject—B. The second procedure lists all examples of subject A together followed by all examples of subject B together.

As we have learned in previous lessons, a well-organized paragraph consists of several types of sentences. We have discussed the function of the topic sentence (TS), the example sentence (E), and the restatement sentence (R). In writing comparison paragraphs, however, additional sentence types may be used. In many paragraphs, for example, a topic introducer (TI) is used. The topic sentence then states more specifically the basis of comparison. Example sentences are, of course, still used but in this lesson will be marked as A-E1, B-E1, A-E2, B-E2, and so on, depending upon which subject the sentence is illustrating. Transition sentences (Tr) may be used to change from one point of view to another, from one set of ideas to another, or from one subject to another.

From Paragraph to Theme

Despite their obvious differences in length, the paragraph and the theme are quite similar structurally. For example, the paragraph is introduced by either a topic sentence or a topic introducer followed by a topic sentence. In the theme, the first paragraph provides introductory material and establishes the topic focus. Next, the sentences comprising the body of a paragraph function as developers of the topic sentence. Similarly, the body of a theme consists of a number of example paragraphs that expand and support the ideas presented in the introductory paragraph. Finally, a terminator—whether a restatement, conclusion, or observation—ends the paragraph. The theme, too, has a device which brings its ideas to a logically and psychologically satisfying completion: the concluding paragraph. Although exceptions to these generalizations may be observed in modern creative writing, most well-written expository paragraphs and themes are comparable in structure.

4.1a Does this paragraph include the necessary parts discussed—topic sentence, developers, terminator? Identify them.
4.1b Classify the paragraph developers according to subject A or subject B. Is there a logical alternation?
4.1c Point out transitional devices—either words or phrases—used in this paragraph.
4.1d Do you think the final sentence is an adequate terminator? Why?

4.2 Read the following paragraph and notice the relationship between the subject A examples and the subject B examples.

The folk sculpture of black Africa has influenced many modern artists. Perhaps the most striking example of this influence is to be found in the obvious relationship between the African primitive artists and the contemporary Spanish genius, Pablo Picasso. Characterized by a bulkiness of form, the sculptures of the Africans appear solid and heavy. Limitations of clay and wood media and simplicity of the artists' tools coupled with an imaginative conception of reality often result in exaggeration of human features. Typically associated with such serious events as reproduction and death, these sculptures nevertheless exhibit to the beholder a light spirit and a sense of humor. Also stressing the themes of love and death, Picasso uses fantastic and grotesque shapes and colors to portray both the beauty and cruelty of human existence. Faces look in two directions; bodies are "all eyes" or "all feet." Seated figures take on the appearance of featureless boulders. Consciously or unconsciously, Picasso and the African artists distort their subjects in similar ways to present a more intense vision of man.

4.2a Identify the topic introducer (TI) and the topic sentence (TS). Explain their relationship.

4.2b What form does this comparison paragraph have? That is, does it alternate examples of subject A and subject B, or does it list all A examples together, followed by all B examples together?

4.2c The examples describing aspects of African sculpture and Picasso's work are similar.

AFRICAN A-E1 "solid and heavy"

E2 "exaggeration of human features"

E3 "serious events . . . light spirit"

PICASSO B-E1 "beauty and cruelty of human existence"

E2 "all eyes" or "all feet"

E3 "featureless boulders"

Notice that the first example under Picasso is similar to the last example under African sculpture. Linking these two examples together makes a smooth transition from subject A to subject B.

The paragraph structure would be represented as follows:

TI / TS / A-E1, E2, E3; B-E1, E2, E3 / R

4.2d Write a title for the paragraph.

4.3 The following paragraph has no terminator. As you read, try to keep the main idea of the paragraph in mind so that you can write an effective restatement sentence.

The Problems and Policies of Black Mayors

Elected in 1968, Carl Stokes and Richard Hatcher, the first black mayors of major U.S. cities, share common problems as well as common policies. Stokes, the mayor of Cleveland, Ohio, won by a narrow margin. Similarly, nearly one-half the voters of Gary, Indiana, opposed Hatcher in the mayoralty election. Stokes must deal with the problems of slums, crime, and air pollution. Hatcher, too, contends with these urban problems in addition to prostitution and gambling. In an attempt to personalize government, Stokes recommends that citizens bring complaints directly to City Hall. With similar strategy, Hatcher has organized MAP, the Mayor's Access Program, which allows city dwellers to contact officials at neighborhood meetings. In addition, Stokes originated the "Cleveland: NOW!" movement, a community-action program designed to aid housing and business. Hatcher, also, has made great strides toward city improvement by attracting over $30 million in

federal and private grants. _____

_____

_____

_____

4.3a What form does this comparison paragraph have? That is, does it alternate examples of subject A and subject B, or does it list all A examples together, followed by all B examples together?
4.3b Are both a topic introducer and a topic sentence used?
4.3c In the space provided, supply a terminator to close the paragraph logically.

4.4 Read the following paragraph. In addition to observing the structure of the paragraph, pay attention to the kind of vocabulary used in a discussion of religions.

Similarities in Christianity and Islam

Two of the major religions of the world are Christianity and Islam. Although seemingly different, the two faiths share several fundamental beliefs and practices. Both worship the same deity, whom the Christians term God and the Muslims call Allah. For knowledge of his faith and for inspiration, the Christian turns to his holy book, the Bible. The Muslim, too, has a holy book, the Koran, which guides his prayers and gives meaning to his life. The Ten Commandments and the Sermon on the Mount provide a code of ethics for the lives of all Christians. Similarly, all Muslims subscribe to the Hadith and the Five Pillars of Faith for daily guidance. Such basic similarities in code and conduct illustrate the shared heritage of Christianity and Islam.

4.4a Discuss the function of each sentence in the paragraph and assign to each an appropriate symbol: TI, TS, A-E . . . , Tr, R. (Exclude sentence number three. Notice that sentence number three is an example of two subjects compared in a single sentence. This is one way of writing comparisons, but it is not emphasized in this lesson. If the sentence were assigned a symbol, it would be labeled as AB.)
4.4b Identify the transitional words or devices used.
4.4c What parallels can you find between the words or phrases of the restatement sentence and those of the topic sentence?
4.4d What meanings do the following words have for you: *inspiration, ethics, heritage, fundamental.*

4.5 As you read the following paragraph, pay particular attention to the example sentences, which constitute the paragraph developers.

Problems of New Immigrants to New York City

Over the past decade Puerto Ricans and Southern blacks have contributed the most significant immigration populations to the New York City area. Both groups come from similar backgrounds and follow similar patterns in trying to adapt to the complexities of city life. As U.S. citizens, Puerto Ricans have the freedom to move from Puerto Rico to any location within the United States. Also as citizens, they have the responsibility of serving in the U.S. armed forces. Set apart from the average New Yorker by physical appearance and language difference, Puerto Ricans are compelled to cluster in certain neighborhoods and become ghetto inhabitants.

The children often arrive educationally disadvantaged due to underdeveloped school systems on the island. The adults generally possess rural skills rather than urban skills. From the rural South, blacks also arrive in the New York City area with skills insufficient to compete in urban life. Their children similarly are educationally handicapped because of separate and inferior schooling. Frequently sharing the same ghettoes with Puerto Ricans, the Southern blacks, with their distinctive speech and obvious physical characteristics, often live together in neighborhoods segregated from those of the white New Yorker. Although they have the rights and responsibilities of U.S. citizenship, including military service, Southern blacks, like Puerto Ricans, find it extremely difficult to achieve full citizenship in a hostile urban environment. Both of these groups share similar socio-economic characteristics and suffer similar problems of adjustment in a technologically oriented urban setting.

4.5a Classify the paragraph developers according to subject A or subject B.

4.5b What parallels can you find between the subject A examples and subject B examples? Notice that the first and second examples under subject A (As U.S. citizens, . . . Also as citizens . . .) are compressed into a single example sentence under subject B (Although they have the rights and responsibilities . . .).

4.5c Does the similarity of ideas in sentences 7 and 8 serve as a transitional device from subject A to subject B? What word ties the two sentences together?

4.5d What symbols would you use to describe the paragraph structure?

4.6 Transition sentences are used in the following paragraph to link each set of comparisons. As you read the paragraph, notice that a viewpoint is stated in a sentence, which is then followed by a subject A example, then a subject B example. Another transition sentence introduces the next set of comparisons.

_____

Modern films and plays often contain famous old literary themes in disguise. *West Side Story,* for example, is a recent musical drama based upon Shakespeare's *Romeo and Juliet.* The young, star-crossed lovers in New York's Puerto Rican district are Maria and Tony. Their ill-fated Shakespearean counterparts are, of course, Romeo and Juliet. Both couples meet and fall in love in the midst of family hostility. Maria's brother, Bernardo, is the leader of a gang which rivals Tony's gang. Juliet's kinsmen, the Capulets, bitterly oppose the Montagues, Romeo's family. Each of the young men is hurried on to his doom by the illusion of his lover's death. Tony believes, because of a deliberately false report, that his lover has been killed. Romeo discovers his lover unconscious and believes her dead. In the end, animosity between the opposing factions causes the death of the innocent lovers. Tony dies in a gang street fight. Romeo and Juliet commit suicide. The similarity between *West Side Story* and *Romeo and Juliet,* as illustrated by these comparisons, is an example of the contemporary use of established literary themes.

4.6a What is the function of the TI?

4.6b How is the TS related to the TI?

4.6c Explain the function of the sentence, "Both couples meet and fall in love in the midst of family hostility."

4.6d Can you point out other sentences in the paragraph that serve the same function as that in 4.6c?

4.6e What is the purpose of a restatement sentence? Is the one used here adequate?

4.6f Notice the use of *star-crossed* to describe Maria and Tony and the use of a similar description—ill-fated—to characterize Romeo and Juliet. In writing a comparison, it is often necessary to use pairs of words conveying similar meanings in order to tighten the comparison, to avoid repetitious statements, or to compare in more subtle ways. Can you point out two or three other such pairs?

4.6g Write a short title for the paragraph. A good title arouses an expectation in the reader that is satisfied by the content of the paragraph.

4.7 Remember that the purpose of a comparison paragraph is to point out the similarities between two subjects. There may be obvious differences between the two subjects, but the similarities are emphasized. With this idea in mind, write two comparison paragraphs on different subjects. The first paragraph should use alternating A and B examples similar to the structure of the model paragraphs 4.1, 4.3, 4.4. The second paragraph should have a series of A examples followed by a series of B examples similar to the structure of the model paragraphs 4.2 or 4.5.

4.7(a)   Name _____ Date _____

4.7(b) Name _____ Date _____

_____

_____

_____

_____

_____

_____

_____

_____

_____

_____

_____

_____

_____

_____

_____

_____

_____

_____

_____

Paragraph Development by Contrast

5

5.1 Unlike the comparison paragraph, which compares similar aspects of two subjects, the contrast paragraph compares dissimilar aspects of two subjects. Like the comparison paragraph, however, two procedures may be followed in writing contrast paragraphs. The first method alternates examples of subject A with examples of subject B. The contrasts may be in the same sentence, or they may be in consecutive sentences. The other method presents all subject A examples together, then all subject B examples together. The symbols used in previous lessons—TI, TS, A-E . . . , B-E . . . , Tr, R—will continue to be used in the structural description of contrast paragraphs.

Where to Study

One major decision which faces the student ready to begin higher education is the choice between the university and the small college. Universities, of course, provide a wide range of departments of specialization, as well as numerous courses within each department. Small colleges, however, offer a better student-faculty ratio, thus allowing individualized attention and more independent research. On the other hand, the numerous cultural and social attractions usually available in large institutions draw students to universities. Although fewer and sometimes less noteworthy, the events held at small colleges nonetheless encourage more direct student involvement and individual participation. Finally, the university closely approximates the real world; it provides a free, impersonal, and anonymous existence. In contrast, the ivory-tower atmosphere of the small college grants the student four years of structured living in which to contemplate and prepare for the real world. In determining his choice of educational institutions, the student must, therefore, consider many factors.

5.1a In writing comparison paragraphs, transitional words such as *similarly, also, too, both* are used. For contrast paragraphs, however, other transitional words and phrases are employed: *unlike, on the other hand, in contrast, however.* Locate the transitional words and phrases used in this paragraph to contrast aspects of the small college and the large university.

5.1b What procedure is used to contrast elements of the two subjects? That is, does the paragraph alternate examples of A and B, or does it list all A examples together, followed by all B examples together?

5.1c What symbols represent the structure of the paragraph? (See

exercise 4.4a.) _____

5.1d Be prepared to discuss in class the meanings of *specialization, interaction, anonymous* (adjective), *anonymity* (noun), *approximate* (adjective), *approximate* (verb).

5.2 Read the following partial paragraph. As you read, try to imagine the kind of statement that would be a good topic sentence for the paragraph. Such a sentence should point out the contrasts between the two subjects discussed.

_____

_____

_____

The astronaut, for example, combats weightlessness, meteor showers, and radiation storms. He confronts the danger of being forever trapped in the gravitational field of another planet. In addition, the complexity of the equipment employed requires the spaceman to be a highly trained technician. In contrast, the sea explorer needed only a rudimentary knowledge of sailing to operate his ship. His greatest worry was falling off the edge of the earth. Further, the natural forces opposing the sea adventurer were storms and days of blistering heat without wind. The type of challenges encountered, as well as time, separate the space traveler and the sea explorer.

5.2a The topic sentence of this paragraph has been omitted. From the three alternatives given, choose the sentence which most effectively establishes the topic of the paragraph and write it in the space provided above. Be prepared to discuss your reasons for eliminating the two other alternatives.

1. Today's spaceman and yesterday's sea explorer faced many hardships.
2. Modern spacemen and ancient sea voyagers have many common problems.
3. The obstacles that today's space explorer faces are considerably different from those the sea voyager met several centuries ago.

5.2b In the space provided directly above the paragraph, supply an appropriate title.

5.2c What procedure has been followed in presenting the examples in this paragraph?

A-E1, E2, E3; B-E1, E2, E3

or

A-E1, B-E1, A-E2, B-E2, A-E3, B-E3

5.2d Identify the transitional words or phrases used.

5.2e Learn the words *technician, rudimentary, obstacles, gravitational.*

5.3 The following paragraph has a topic introducer, but the topic sentence has been omitted. As you read, try to imagine how the main contrasting ideas could be expressed in a topic sentence.

Cultural Differences Between the United States and Spain

One fascinating benefit of travel to foreign places is learning how customs differ from country to country. _____

_____

_____

_____

_____

In the United States, for example, many clubs exist for people with similar recreational, occupational, or religious interests. In Spain, however, the basic social unit is still the family. Another difference involves the work day. Most American businesses operate continuously during the day, allowing only 45 minutes or an hour for lunch. Traditional Spanish firms, on the other hand, usually close for a two- or three-hour period each afternoon to allow workers to go home for a meal. Still another contrast concerns student life. While most American students work part-time or full-time during the school year and during vacations, it is relatively uncommon for Spanish students to be employed. These observations are just a few samples of the many differences between life in Spain and life in the United States.

5.3a Write an original TS in the space provided. Remember that a TS serves to give a specific focus to the contrasts suggested in the TI.
5.3b Identify transitional words and phrases, and explain how they relate the ideas involved.

5.4 The sentences listed below are *not* arranged in either of the two logical contrast paragraph patterns. Study the sentences carefully and try to decide which sentence is the TS, which sentences state contrasts and in what order, and which sentence is the R.

____   His narrowly educated counterpart, however, is rarely at ease with subjects ranging from music to philosophy to geology.

____   The specially trained student, in contrast, enters a position with knowledge that can be applied immediately.

____   One of the major disputes in education today is the controversy over specialization and liberal arts.

____   Each educational approach offers both advantages and disadvantages to students.

____   For employment purposes, on the other hand, the liberal arts student usually must be trained for a specific position once hired.

____   The graduate of a liberal arts college can boast a familiarity with numerous academic disciplines.

5.4a Write a number (1 through 6) before each sentence to show its logical position in a well-ordered contrast paragraph.
5.4b Read the sentences in the arrangement you have established in order to experience the paragraph as a unified whole.
5.4c Using symbols, give the paragraph structure as you have

arranged the sentences in 5.4a. _____
5.4d Identify the transitional devices used.
5.4e Write a title for the paragraph.
5.4f Be prepared to define and explain the words *counterpart, controversy* (noun), *controversial* (adjective), *discipline* (noun, several meanings), *discipline* (verb), *disciplinary* (adjective).

5.5 As you read the following incomplete paragraph, notice that the two sets of contrast sentences are introduced by transitional devices that enumerate. Such words or phrases—*first, second, third, fourth; in the first place, in the second place, in the third place*—could go on indefinitely. You could continue to write *in the nineteenth place, in the twentieth place, in the twenty-first place,* and so on. In common practice, however, you seldom should go beyond the second or third place. After you read the paragraph, you will be expected to complete the paragraph in two steps.

Contrast Between Two Recent Wars

Today, as in the 1940's, American soldiers are engaged in battle. Great differences exist, however, between World War II and the conflict in Vietnam. In the first place, World War II was a declared war. The Vietnamese encounter, on the other hand, has never been officially declared as a war by Congress, nor is it ever likely to be. In the second place, World War II involved many countries and included numerous theaters of battle in Europe, North Africa, Asia, and the Pacific. The present conflict, in contrast, is a relatively contained encounter, involving mainly American and

Vietnamese troops within the confines of Vietnam. _____

_____

_____

_____

_____

_____

_____

_____

_____

_____

_____

_____

_____

_____

5.5a In the space provided, write two sets of contrast sentences (four sentences) that illustrate the differences between World War II and the Vietnamese war. Remember to use transitional devices; introduce one set of contrast sentences with *further,* another set with *and finally.*

5.5b Write a terminator to conclude the paragraph effectively.

5.5c What symbols would you use to describe the structure of the

completed paragraph? _____

5.6 Write two contrast paragraphs on topics of your choice. The first paragraph should alternate A and B examples. The second should list together all examples illustrating subject A, then all examples illustrating subject B.

5.6(a) Name_____ Date_____

_____

_____

_____

_____

_____

_____

_____

_____

_____

_____

_____

_____

_____

_____

_____

_____

_____

_____

_____

_____

5.6(b)   Name_____ Date_____

_____

Theme Development by Comparison and Contrast

6.1 Often a writer may want to describe several aspects of two subjects that have both similarities and differences. For this purpose, the sentence developers of a paragraph or the paragraph developers of a theme may employ the combined techniques of comparison and contrast. As you read the following paragraph, carefully examine the sets of sentences that compare or contrast aspects of the two subjects being discussed.

Two Black Giants of the Turn of the Century

Two black leaders who have continued to influence black American thinking since the late nineteenth century are Booker T. Washington and W. E. B. DuBois. An examination of their lives reveals both similarities and differences in their family background, professional education and careers, social ideology, and influence on black America. [Washington, born a plantation slave of mixed parentage, received his education and spent his life in the South. Like Washington, DuBois was of mixed ancestry, but he was born free and lived in the different racial atmosphere of New England.] After completing his

college degree and following a brief teaching career, Washington
was chosen to start a black normal school which became Tuskegee
Institute. DuBois, after his education at Fisk and later at Harvard
where he received a Ph.D., taught at Wilburforce College and for
many years at Atlanta University. Washington's work at Tuskegee
reflected his strong belief in self-help for blacks through training in
trades and skills which would make them economically indispensable to the white community. DuBois, too, recognized the need for
economic advancement of the black, but he favored the formation
of a college-educated black elite that could lead the race to
socio-political equality as well as economic betterment. As some
modern black leaders still do, Washington emphasized patience and
warned against the use of violence in the acquisition of civil rights.
DuBois, however, called for immediate voting privileges and took a
position, also held by some modern leaders, that would not
denounce the use of force in the attainment of what he called
"full manhood rights." Both Booker T. Washington and W. E. B.
DuBois have had lasting influence on black America, but even a
superficial examination of their lives reveals differences as well as
similarities in their backgrounds and in the development of their
persuasive ideologies.

6.1a What symbols would you use to describe the functions of

the first two sentences in the paragraph? _____
These two sentences make up a set which introduces the main idea
of the paragraph.
6.1b The next eight sentences in the paragraph have the function
of subject developers. They are to be looked at as four sets of two
sentences each. Sometimes the two sentences of a set are
comparison sentences; sometimes they are contrast sentences.
Reread the two sentences in the paragraph inside brackets [ ].
Why do these two sentences make up a set? How are these
sentences related to each other?
6.1c Place brackets [ ] around each of the three remaining sets in
the paragraph.
6.1d In two to four words, what aspect of the lives of Washington
and DuBois is discussed in each set of sentences?

1. _____ family background

2. _____

3. _____

4. _____

6.1e The last sentence in this paragraph is a restatement sentence. What function does it play in the paragraph?

6.1f This paragraph, like all well-written paragraphs, has introducers, developers, and a terminator.

How many sets of sentences are introducers?   ____

How many sets of sentences are subject developers?   ____

How many sentences are terminators?   ____

If this paragraph were expanded into a theme,
  how many paragraphs would you write?   ____

6.1g Learn to spell, pronounce, and use the following words: *ideology, parentage, indispensable, elite, attainment, persuasive.*

6.2 As you read the following theme, try to think about its plan of organization. Keep in mind that it is an expansion of paragraph 6.1.

Two Black Giants of the Turn of the Century

____   Two black leaders who have continued to influence black American thinking since the late nineteenth century are Booker T. Washington and W. E. B. DuBois. Born only twelve years apart, sharing the same racial heritage, and envisioning the same goals for blacks, these dynamic men were a world apart in their feeling for what were the appropriate methods for attaining these goals. An examination of their lives, consequently, reveals both similarities and differences in their family backgrounds, professional education and careers, social ideology, and influence on black America.

_____ The family backgrounds of the two men show obvious parallels but also striking differences. Washington, of mixed parentage, was born a plantation slave in 1856 in Franklin County, Virginia. After the Emancipation, he moved to Malden, West Virginia, where he led a life of poverty, attending school at night and working during the day to support members of his family. He spent most of his life in the South, receiving his education there and devoting his adult years to the education of others. Also of mixed ancestry, DuBois, on the other hand, was born free in 1868 in Great Barrington, Massachusetts, an entirely different racial environment. Educated in the South, the North, and abroad, he spent his adult years in the North, in cosmopolitan Atlanta, and in traveling throughout the world. Early environment and experience of both Washington and DuBois, at some points similar and at some points different, shaped their characters and formed their expectations for their race.

_____ It was through their education that both leaders were able to pursue careers that frequently led them along similar paths but, just as frequently, forced them to take different directions. Washington, with the help of a sponsor, was able to further his education by attending Hampton Institute in Virginia. Upon graduation, he returned to Malden, where he taught for two years. After a brief period of study at Wayland Seminary in Washington, D.C., he was invited to return to Hampton as an instructor. He remained there only two years, but during that short time he helped develop a successful experimental education program for American Indians and established a night school. In 1881, Washington was chosen to start a black normal school, Tuskegee Institute, of which he later became president. His entire professional career was spent in helping this institution and the people it served. DuBois, too, was sponsored in his education—first at Fisk, then at Harvard, where he received a Ph.D. After a brief period of post-doctoral study at the University of Berlin, DuBois began his teaching career at Wilburforce College in Ohio, where he stayed for two years. During much of the remainder of his life, he devoted his talents to educating others either through his teaching at Atlanta University, through his writing, or through his work with the NAACP. Although they at times perceived different goals and took different routes, both educators dedicated their lives to the service of their people.

     An investigation of the ideologies of Washington and DuBois yields several points of agreement as well as numerous divergences. Both men emphasized self-help for blacks. Both recognized the need for economic advancement. The two spokesmen disagreed, however, over the purpose of higher education. According to pragmatist Washington, blacks should be trained in trades and skills that would make them economically indispensable to the white community. An idealist and intellectual, DuBois advocated the formation of a college-educated black elite, the "Talented Tenth," which could lead the race to socio-political equality as well as economic betterment. Another subject of disagreement concerned voting rights. Whereas Washington preached patience in the acquisition of the right to vote, DuBois insisted upon immediate enfranchisement in order to secure other civil rights. Despite early similarities, it is in the development of their social ideologies, then, that major differences between the two men begin to appear.

     Both Washington and DuBois, irrespective of their differences in ideologies, have had significant impact on persons most directly involved in America's racial problems. Through his role as an educator, Washington considerably influenced the blacks of his time. He was, nevertheless, opposed by many intellectuals for his emphasis on vocational or trade school education, which would enable the black to be a member of the labor force but not of management. Washington's life and beliefs have continued to influence the black and white communities. As some modern black leaders still do, he emphasized patience and warned against the use of violence in the acquisition of civil rights. DuBois, on the other hand, called for immediate voting privileges and took a position, also held by some contemporary black activists, that would not denounce the use of force in the attainment of what he called "full manhood rights." With his strong educational background and first-hand knowledge gained through wide travels in Asia and Africa, he brought a formidable intellectual presence to his academic tasks and the nonacademic organizations in which he participated. DuBois broke with the NAACP, which he helped found, when the organization would not take a firm position on economic issues during the depression of the 1930's. He returned to the organization later when he retired from teaching. An activist to the end, he helped circulate the Stockholm Peace Petition in the U.S. and was awarded the Lenin Peace Prize in 1959. His Marxist interpretation of the blacks' struggle for fair treatment made him a controversial but influential spokesman. Each man, in his own way, helped initiate the directions of contemporary black thought regarding the best means to solve racial inequities.

_____   Both Washington and DuBois were highly respected leaders of their time, whose philosophies were articulated so clearly that they continue to influence contemporary thought. Their family backgrounds and educational experiences led them to formulate goals, ideals, and methods which have had lasting influence on black America. But even a superficial examination of·their lives reveals differences as well as similarities in their backgrounds and in the development of their persuasive ideologies.

6.2a Label each paragraph in the model theme using the symbols TP (for topic paragraph), CP (for comparison or contrast paragraph), and RP (for restatement paragraph). Since there are several CP's, number them consecutively CP1, CP2, and so on.

6.2b Underline the sentence that states the main point in CP1. Does the main point of this paragraph come first in the paragraph?

6.2c What form does CP1 have? That is, does it alternate examples A and B, or does it list all A examples together, followed by all B examples together?

6.2d Underline the sentences that state the main point in CP2, CP3, and CP4. Do the main points of these paragraphs come first?

6.2e What relationship do the unmarked sentences in each comparison or contrast paragraph have to the underlined sentence in that paragraph?

6.2f Which single sentence in the RP serves best to round off the whole theme by referring back to the topic paragraph?

6.2g Learn to spell, pronounce, and use the following words: *envisioning, cosmopolitan, divergences, pragmatist, enfranchisement, articulated.*

6.2h Now read model paragraph 6.1 again to discover the relationship between the paragraph and the theme. Notice that the sets of sentences you bracketed in exercise 6.1f were expanded into the CP's in the theme.

6.3 As you read the following paragraph, try to think of ways the various sets of sentences could be expanded into separate paragraphs to form a theme.

Two Black Giants of the 1960's

The two leaders who exerted the greatest influence on black social thought and action in the 1960's were Malcolm X and Martin Luther King, Jr. A comparison of the lives and careers of these two architects of contemporary black activism reveals both similarities and differences in background, education, ideology, and impact. Born in Omaha in 1925, Malcolm Little grew up in the streets of Boston and New York after the murder of his father, a Baptist preacher, and subsequent mental illness of his mother. Martin Luther King, Jr., born in Atlanta in 1929, son of a highly respected Baptist pastor, grew up in the relative security of the black middle class. Young Malcolm received his education in the gutters of the ghetto, in reform school, and in prison. In contrast, Martin, as a son of educated parents, grew up in a stable environment that stimulated his academic interests, leading him eventually tc Boston College, where he earned a Ph.D. After several years in prison, Little became a minister of the Black Muslims and as Malcolm X espoused militant black solidarity and separatism. King, on the other hand, as a Christian minister advocated the solution of racial injustices through nonviolence, cooperation, and love. Since his assassination in 1965, Malcolm X has continued to gain stature among the advocates of a black revolution. Slain in 1968, Martin Luther King as spokesman for racial justice through nonviolence has also continued to inspire many Americans. These two black giants of the 1960's exhibit both similarities and differences in their lives and careers, but their martyrdom in trying to achieve a better life for blacks has continued to motivate the followers of their conflicting methods and aspirations.

6.3a Place brackets [ ] around each set of comparison or contrast sentences. How many sets have you bracketed?

6.3b In previous exercises we have studied paragraph organization in some detail. The following diagram may help you visualize the process of expanding the paragraph into a theme employing the same method of organization. The first column identifies the purpose of individual sentences with the appropriate symbol. The second column indicates the function of the sets of sentences. The third column represents the expansion of the sets of sentences into paragraphs within a theme.

Paragraph level	Function	Theme level
TI / TS "Malcolm & Martin"	INTRODUCERS ⟹	TP
A-E1, B-E1 "background"	DEVELOPERS ⟹	CP1
A-E2, B-E2 "education"	DEVELOPERS ⟹	CP2
A-E3, B-E3 "ideology"	DEVELOPERS ⟹	CP3
A-E4, B-E4 "impact"	DEVELOPERS ⟹	CP4
R "Malcolm & Martin"	TERMINATOR ⟹	RP

6.3c Using the procedure illustrated in 6.1 and 6.2, expand the sentences of this paragraph into a theme with the structure TP / CP1, CP2, CP3, CP4 / RP. Give the theme a title.

For additional information about the lives of these two men, you might refer to the following:

1. Louis E. Lomax. *To Kill a Black Man.* Los Angeles: Holloway Publishing House, 1968.
2. Autobiographies and other writings of Malcolm X and Martin Luther King, Jr.
3. Recent biographies of the two men.

Paragraph Development by Definition

7

7.1 Read the model paragraph. As you read, pay close attention to both the meaning and the organization of the ideas discussed.

The Definition Paragraph

A definition paragraph describes, explains, or defines an unfamiliar term by relating that which is unknown to that which is already known. It makes use of the techniques of comparison, contrast, and synthesis. More specifically, a definition paragraph may be developed *positively* by using sentences that show that an unknown term is the same as or *like* some known term. Or it may be developed *negatively* by using sentences that show that an unknown term, though similar in some respects, is basically *unlike* some known term. Or it may be developed *synthetically* by *bringing together* the appropriate positive and negative characteristics of one or more similar terms to form a new concept. In any case a given definition paragraph whether developed positively, negatively, or synthetically, normally ends with a sentence that summarizes the distinctive features of the term being defined.

7.1a What three techniques may a definition paragraph use? (See sentence 2 in the model paragraph.)

7.1b Which sentence explains the technique of synthesis?

7.1c Discuss the terms *synthesis* and *synthetically* as they are used in developing a definition paragraph. What meaning of the word *synthetic* did you already know?

7.1d What is the function of a terminator in a definition paragraph?

7.1e The techniques of comparison, contrast, and synthesis may be observed in the table below. A partial list of defining characteristics is given in the center column. This list might serve alone as a satisfactory definition through synthesis, but additional information could be provided through comparison and contrast. For instance, a magazine is both similar to and different from a book and a newspaper. *Like* qualities are indicated as + and *unlike* qualities are indicated as – in the chart. Study these characteristics and discuss other qualities which could be added to the list.

Known Term: book	*Unknown Term: magazine*	*Known Term: newspaper*
+	printed pages	+
–	slick thin paper	–
+	cover	–
+	bound	–
+	use of colored pictures	–
–	advertisements	+
–	multiple authorship	+
–	published regularly	+
–	published weekly	+
–	published monthly	–

7.2 The definition paragraph is often used at the beginning of a longer paper or book to define a new subject. A biology textbook might open with a definition paragraph explaining the term *biology*. Definition paragraphs also serve sometimes as summaries of longer essays or chapters. If the purpose of a chapter in your biology text is to explain or describe the concept of photosynthesis, the final paragraph may be a short definition summarizing the major characteristics of photosynthesis. In a discussion of the political relationship between the United States and Puerto Rico, for example, an opening paragraph might be a definition of *commonwealth* as this term applies to Puerto Rico.

The Commonwealth of Puerto Rico

Since 1952, Puerto Rico has been a commonwealth, with characteristics similar to and different from both states and territories of the United States. Basically, the citizens of the Puerto Rican commonwealth have all the rights and obligations of U.S. citizens except for the right to vote in presidential elections and the obligation to pay federal income taxes. Like state governments, the government of Puerto Rico is autonomous, with its own elected governor, Senate, and House of Representatives. Some of the territories, on the other hand, have governors appointed by the President of the United States. Unlike the fifty states, Puerto Rico has representation in the U.S. Congress only through a nonvoting resident commissioner. Some of the territories have similar representation, but others have none. With the territories and states, Puerto Rico shares U.S. citizenship and a common monetary system, and comes under jurisdiction of the U.S. Constitution. Unlike the territories, however, its citizens must serve in the armed forces, and unlike the fifty states, it cannot maintain its own militia. Although its economy is integrated with that of the U.S., it does not always share equally with the states in benefits from legislation that extends economic assistance to veterans, farmers, school children, and the aged. Because of its peculiar status as a commonwealth, it has a fiscal autonomy unlike the territories and

a cultural autonomy unlike any of the states. _____

_____

_____

_____

_____

7.2a In the space provided in the model paragraph, supply a terminator to logically summarize the paragraph.

7.2b Be prepared to explain the meaning of the words *fiscal, autonomy, autonomous, jurisdiction,* and *militia* as they are used in paragraph 7.2.

7.2c Using the information given in paragraph 7.2, prepare a table similar to the one in 7.1e, listing characteristics of a commonwealth in the center column, and the comparison of states and territories on either side.

Name _____ Date _____

Known Term: state	Unknown Term: commonwealth	Known Term: territory
_____	_____	_____
_____	_____	_____
_____	_____	_____
_____	_____	_____
_____	_____	_____
_____	_____	_____
_____	_____	_____
_____	_____	_____
_____	_____	_____
_____	_____	_____
_____	_____	_____
_____	_____	_____
_____	_____	_____
_____	_____	_____
_____	_____	_____
_____	_____	_____
_____	_____	_____

7.2d In comparing a commonwealth with both states and territories, paragraph 7.2 is longer than model paragraph 7.1 or those that
follow in this lesson. Rewrite paragraph 7.2, leaving out all references
to territories, so that your paragraph defines by relating only two
terms. Notice that you will need some new transitional devices and a
different terminator.

7.2d(a)   Name _____ Date _____

_____

7.3 Definition paragraphs are often used to explain a general concept by using a specific example or occurrence of the concept.

The El Yunque Rain Forest

A rain forest, as the term suggests, is a kind of wooded area, subject to unusually heavy and frequent rains. Found only in the tropical or subtropical regions of the Caribbean, Brazil, Africa, and Asia, rain forests contain a great variety of trees including bamboo, palm, cedar, ebony, calabash, and whitewood. Many of these trees grow to a height of more than a hundred feet, with dense canopies or crowns characteristically forming three distinguishable stories. Although ground flora is sparse, climbers of all kinds abound, and often exotic flowers appear inconspicuously in the thick foliage. This luxuriant growth results from an annual rainfall in excess of ninety inches, with no dry season. A rain forest of spectacular beauty covers El Yunque, a mountain just outside San Juan, Puerto Rico. The El Yunque rain forest—average rainfall 180 inches per year—is filled with lush, tropical greenery, millions of tiny wild orchids, thirty-foot ferns, and hundreds of varieties of trees and plants, all growing in native splendor.

7.3a The term *rain forest,* defined in this paragraph, is a compound of two familiar words. How are the ideas represented by these two words expanded in the second part of sentence 1?

7.3b Which part of the compound term is developed in sentences 2, 3, and 4? How is this development accomplished?

7.3c Does sentence 5 deal with the same part of the compound term as sentences 2, 3, and 4? How are the two parts of the compound term tied together in sentence 5?

7.3d The first five sentences of the paragraph describe some of the general characteristics of a rain forest. What do sentences 6 and 7 describe?

7.3e In what way does sentence 7 summarize the whole paragraph?

7.3f Previous lessons have made use of special symbols to represent the functions of sentences within a paragraph or of paragraphs within a theme. These symbols help you visualize the structure or organization of a paragraph or a theme without longwinded explanations. Symbols make it easier to separate the *function* of an example sentence (E1, E2, E3, E4), for instance, from the *subject matter* (education, background, ideology, career). In themselves, symbols are of little importance; the symbol (TS) or the label (topic sentence) merely gives us a way of discussing the writing process. It is easier to understand the concept *topic sentence* and to discuss its relationship to the function of other sentences in a paragraph apart from the subject of that sentence. Hopefully, by this time, you are able to think of the organization or method of development of a paragraph or a theme at the same time you think about the subject matter you are reading. Although symbols are used sparingly in the remainder of your textbook, you may find it helpful to continue to write the symbols for the model paragraphs or themes as you study them. Modify the symbols you have already learned or invent new ones to represent effectively the new methods of development introduced in the remainder of the lessons.

Use the symbols you have already learned or invent new ones to describe the structure of the model paragraph in 7.3.

7.4   Use of the following term is so common and widespread that it is often no longer explained in the news media. It is doubtful, however, that most readers know precisely what it means.

The Barrio

Barrio is a Spanish word borrowed recently into English and used both in scholarly writing and journalistic reporting and commentary. In Spanish, *barrio* means neighborhood or is used to refer to the area or vicinity around some landmark such as a church or town hall. In some Latin American cities, the barrio is the place where you grew up, where you formed strong family ties, where you made your closest friends. Picked up by the news media in the United States, the term has begun to take on some of the negative characteristics associated with the words *slum* and *ghetto*. For the general American reader or listener, the term *barrio* identifies a Spanish neighborhood of poverty and squalor, and frequently trouble. The barrio in the United States may be the place where the Spanish speaker was born, but it's the neighborhood where most Puerto Ricans, or Cubans, or Mexicans live, whether by choice or economic necessity. Increasingly, the word is used by Spanish-Americans in the United States to identify a unified neighborhood made up of people with the same language, similar social problems, shared aspirations, and an aggressive identification with their origins.

7.4a In paragraph 7.1 the unfamiliar term *definition paragraph* is defined or explained in the first sentence. Read it again. Is the unfamiliar term *barrio* defined in the first sentence of paragraph 7.4? What is the function of sentence 1?

7.4b Words are borrowed from other languages into English because they are useful. Does this definition paragraph give you any clues as to why *barrio* is a useful word in American English, especially in such places as Los Angeles, Chicago, New York, Miami?

7.4c Words borrowed from a foreign language into English often acquire slightly different meanings as they are used by Americans. Discuss the differences in the meaning of *barrio* as it is used in Spanish and in American English.

7.4d The final sentence indicates that the meaning of *barrio* for Spanish-Americans residing in the United States may not be the same for Spanish speakers living elsewhere. In what way may the meaning be different?

7.4e The transitional devices in 7.4 usually indicate *where* or *by what persons* the word *barrio* is used; for example, sentence 2 says *In Spanish.* Pick out the transitional phrases in the remaining sentences.

7.5 Obsolete words such as *charnel house,* newly created words such as *aquanaut,* or foreign words such as *kibbutz,* frequently require definition by means of another familiar word, a sentence, a paragraph, or a longer explanation. The six sentences below, which are printed in a scrambled sequence, if rearranged would constitute a definition paragraph. In the spaces at the left, put the numbers of the sentences in the sequence in which they would occur in a well-ordered paragraph. The paragraph will then explain a foreign word which has no exact English equivalent.

Machismo

____   The word comes from the Spanish *macho* meaning male, but with more of the animal strength and virility than the English word suggests.

____   The combination of courageous behavior and earthy sexuality that characterizes Latin American manliness is called *machismo*.

____   The concept carries the underlying, but usually unstated, notion of sexual potency and even sexual prowess.

____   He is boss in his own home, holds his own in manly conversation and activities, defies authority when his individual masculinity is threatened, is stoic in pain, and meets physical danger with aggressive bravery.

____   It also suggests the proper role of a man, in relation to his family and to the community.

____   Rugged individual courage and primitive sexual energy in a man, from the barrio boaster to the national folk hero, are the principal qualities in the concept *machismo*.

7.5a Discuss with your teacher and your classmates your reasons for arranging the sentences in the sequence you determined.

7.5b Read the sentences in the arrangement you have established in order to experience the paragraph as a unified whole.

7.5c What are the two main characteristics of *machismo?* Which sentence in the model paragraph indicates this?

7.5d Which sentences relate more to the first characteristic? Which to the second?

7.5e What is the transitional word that leads you from the first characteristic to the second characteristic?

7.5f How does the final sentence function as a terminator?

7.5g Discuss the words *virility, potency, prowess, stoic,* and *aggressive bravery.*

7.6 It is often helpful before starting a written assignment to talk through a subject with your classmates and teacher. When the discussion is orderly and systematic, resulting in a patterned sequence of ideas, it may be called an oral composition. Your teacher can help guide the discussion or summarize the discussion, to create an oral composition similar to the written organization stressed in the model paragraphs or themes.

Discuss the term *silent majority* with your classmates and teacher. Your discussion should result in a number of ideas that could become a written definition. The following questions may help get you started:

What do people mean when they say *silent majority?*
What are some of the characteristics of a silent majority?
To what people would you apply this term?
Is the term generally understood by most people?
Is there a term that means the same or nearly the same?
Is there a term that means the opposite?

7.7 Write a definition paragraph based on the class discussion of the term *silent majority.*

_____

_____

_____

_____

_____

_____

_____

_____

_____

_____

_____

_____

_____

_____

_____

_____

_____

7.8 Choose one of the topics listed below and discuss it with your classmates or friends. Write a definition paragraph using one or more of the techniques—comparison, contrast, synthesis—illustrated in this lesson.

Women's Lib	Chicano	Gaucho
Americanized	Racism	Generation Gap
	"Beating the System"	

7.8(a) Name_____ Date_____

_____

_____

_____

_____

_____

_____

_____

_____

_____

_____

_____

_____

_____

_____

_____

_____

_____

_____

_____

Paragraph Development by Classification

8

8.1 Read the following model paragraph.

The Classification of Paragraphs

Individual paragraphs—the building blocks of themes, articles, chapters, and other longer papers—may be classified in a variety of ways. At the theme level, paragraphs may be sorted into functional groups such as introductory, developmental, transitional, summarizing, and the like. Depending upon the purpose or intent of the writer, particular paragraphs may be thought of as aiming to persuade, inform, argue, or excite. Paragraphs may also be classified according to such techniques of development as comparison, contrast, and definition. Another developmental technique might also be the classification paragraph, which organizes items or ideas to be discussed into relatively homogeneous groups. Such classifications make it possible to talk about a large number of paragraphs by grouping them into a small number of classes.

8.1a Does this paragraph illustrate the developmental technique of *classification?* What is discussed or classified in the paragraph?

8.1b Which sentence in the paragraph best defines a classification paragraph?

8.1c In sentence 3, one way of classifying paragraphs is mentioned. What do you think of the approach mentioned in sentence 3 as a means of teaching and learning concrete writing techniques?

8.1d Have you found the techniques suggested in sentences 4 and 5 helpful to you in improving your own writing skills? In what ways?

8.2 Although the following paragraph is long, it clearly identifies four classes of words. As you read, observe how the discussion of each class is developed.

Four Classes of Words

As imprecise or gross as classifications sometimes are, they usually indicate classes, or categories, and labels for these classes that make information more manageable. Frequently, these labels for classes tell us how we are supposed to feel toward a certain thing. The older dictionaries, for example, classified words and assigned them labels such as *vulgar, dialect, colloquial,* and *slang.* Many commonly used words were labeled *vulgar* and in some dictionaries *low,* implying that only the lowest sort of person used such words. This class of words included most of the "four-letter words" associated with the bodily functions of sex and elimination. The class of words called *dialect* included expressions commonly used by certain national groups of people or certain regions of the country. People often inferred from the word *dialect* that the English language was improperly learned or used by these speakers; certainly one would not use such a word beyond the borders of that community. *Colloquial* was a less severe label, but it identified words and expressions that might be used in informal educated speech with friends at school but definitely not in formal compositions. The huge class named *slang* usually meant any word a student used that the teacher did not know, a word understood only a select group of people. Often slang words are quickly forgotten, but they are occasionally taken up by the whole country and soon lose their distinction as slang. The greater social freedom of the past two decades and the language of public protest have liberated words from such rigid classifications. Modern dictionaries reflect this variety of usage by employing few classifications that imply social or moral judgment.

8.2a What additional information would you need to write a definition paragraph about the term *colloquial?*

8.2b What is the topic sentence in this paragraph?

8.2c How might the use of a great number of words from these four classes in your writing limit or restrict communication?

8.2d Check the following words or expressions in at least two different unabridged dictionaries. Give the usage label for each word or phrase.

smidgin	stew in his own juice
lox	rap
bum	up tight
fuck	chippy
smearcase	come off it
stoned	shit
pissed	bird
poontang	screwed up

Do different dictionaries assign different classifications to the same word or expression? Are there words or expressions in this list that are not found in your dictionaries?

8.2e Even though academic writing has become more liberalized, it seldom uses the vulgar class of words. They are used almost without reservation in fiction and in the underground press. They are used less often in the liberal journals. They are used rarely or not at all in the printed mass media of newspapers, news magazines, and picture magazines, except perhaps in direct quotation or in discussion of the words themselves. The editorial mechanics for using such words cover a wide range of possibilities: (1) simply printing the word in its full form; (2) printing only a portion of the word; e.g., "Don't f--k around with that car," in a context that easily reveals the word to anyone who has never heard it but supposedly protects the innocent; (3) printing only the first letter, if the context is clear; e.g., "Get your f___ shoes off the couch"; and (4) omitting the word entirely; e.g., a recent news account of a trial referred to crucial testimony about the use of a word which the newspapers referred to as "... a four-letter word used by many people in referring to the action of sexual intercourse."

As you read various kinds of articles, interviews, news stories, and reports, be on the alert for the devices used by editors in handling these words.

8.3 The following paragraph is written in a very informal style. Like the other model paragraphs in this lesson, it employs the technique of paragraph development by classification.

The people I actually hate are too numerous to list. I can put them into a few categories though. First is the pompous ass. He's the kind of person who comes from Mobile but tries to sound as if he's from Massachusetts. He has the best education money can buy, but he can't remember what he majored in. He insists on paying for every round of drinks and saying, "I remember how it was when I was your age." He's the kind of man who calls his

mother and says, "Hello, Mom, this is *Dr.* Dullard."_____

_____

_____

_____

_____

_____

_____

_____

_____

_____

Third is the junior executive. He never makes a decision; he makes a *critical decision*. He never attends a meeting; he attends a *high-level conference*. He never sends a note; he sends a *memorandum*. And he *never* goes to the john.

8.3a The type of writing you have studied and practiced so far in this book is a rather formal style of expository prose. The use of this style of writing is likely to lead to greater success in school. It might be characterized as *academic* prose. Not all expository writing has such a serious purpose or formal style. The methods of development, nonetheless, in both formal and informal writing are often the same. What makes paragraph 8.3 informal?
8.3b Which sentences tell you that this is going to be a classification paragraph? How do they tell you?
8.3c Write three or four sentences in the blanks provided, characterizing one class of people you dislike. Begin with the transition word *second*.
8.3d In the space provided directly above the paragraph, supply an appropriate title.

8.4 Notice the use of transitional devices in the following model of a classification paragraph.

Birth Control Through Contraception

When the intra-uterine loop contraceptive was being publicized for use in India, huge billboards in the heavily populated urban areas announced, "Loop before you leap." The loop is just one of several types of birth-control methods used today. Three broad classifications of birth-control methods are those that inhibit pregnancies physically, mechanically, or chemically. The oldest method, and perhaps the surest, is abstinence. We generally think of birth-control methods, however, as those that both permit the pleasures of sexual intercourse and prevent the consequences of unwanted pregnancies. One such method is the so-called rhythm method, which permits intercourse during certain safe periods of the menstrual cycle but requires abstinence during unsafe periods when fertilization could occur. More recent methods belonging to this class are the various surgical operations that permit sexual intercourse but do not allow sperm to reach the egg for conception. Various mechanical devices for the same purpose, as well as for preventing the spread of venereal disease, have been made and no doubt cheerfully tested by the inventors. Made first of animal membrane and later of rubber, they have a long history. The loop also belongs to this class of mechanical devices, but its function is totally different. If effective, however, it has the same result: it does not allow pregnancy to occur. The most revolutionary method of birth control is the pill, a contraceptive device that inhibits pregnancy through the chemical changes in the user's body. The ingenuity of research chemists continues in this area through experimentation with once-a-month pills, inoculations, and pills for men. Man's lustful nature supports the modern slogan—better living through chemistry.

8.4a What three means of physically inhibiting pregnancy are mentioned in the first class of birth-control methods?
8.4b Underline the transitional device used to introduce the second class of birth-control methods; to introduce the third class.
8.4c The style of this paragraph mixes a few lines of a light humorous style with a more serious academic prose. Bracket [ ] the sentences or phrases meant to keep the paragraph from becoming too serious. You should find three such examples.

8.5 The following paragraph is taken from the second edition of a popular textbook published in several languages in addition to English. It classifies the various activities of the psychologist into three major enterprises.

Psychology, as defined, comprises a number of different kinds of enterprises, so different that they may seem to have nothing in common. One psychologist is engaged in vocational guidance; he spends his day talking to high school students, studying their academic records and their test scores and from these, in principle, showing the student how to clarify his own ideas about his future training and occupation. Another spends his day studying delayed reaction in goldfish or the navigation of bats. Other psychologists are assisting in the diagnosis of neurotic patients, doing research on

Donald Olding Hebb. *A Textbook of Psychology.* Second Edition. Philadelphia: W. B. Saunders Company, 1966, page 310.

the childhood experiences that contribute to neurosis, or taking part in combined research on the effects of tranquilizers. But all such disparate activities have this in common, that the methods derive from the same fundamental training in the procedures and conceptions of academic psychology, and that the worker is either putting the conceptions to practical use or trying to improve on them (or both).

8.5a Which sentence explains what various psychologists' activities have in common?

8.5b The three classes of psychologists' work are not clearly named in the paragraph. Discuss the activities of each class to determine what distinguishes one from another.

8.5c Indicate the phrase that relates the topic introducer and the terminator in this paragraph.

8.5d Using a good dictionary, decide what less formal words or expressions might be substituted for the following words in the model paragraph: *comprises, enterprises, neurosis, disparate, conceptions.*

8.6 Remember that the purpose of a classification paragraph is to group a large number of items or ideas into a small number of classes. With this in mind, write two classification paragraphs on different subjects. The first paragraph should use an informal style of first person observations, such as, "I believe there are only three types of teachers in the world." (Review 8.3.) The second paragraph should use a more formal academic style. (Review 8.1, 8.2.)

Name_____ Date _____

Theme Development by Definition and Classification

9

9.1 Often a writer employs more than one method of development in a theme. He may, for instance, decide to *classify* objects, events, or terms in order to make it easier for his reader to retain a few classes rather than many specific items. Additionally, he may need to *define* the labels he uses in classifying his subject, especially if these labels are not widely known or are abstract.

The following theme combines the techniques of definition and classification to discuss the contemporary social status of Spanish-Americans living in the United States. After you have read the theme once, reread each paragraph carefully to determine the method of development used.

Spanish-Americans in the United States

Spanish-Americans in the United States are engaged in a new drive to gain their share of the "American dream." In some respects, they are farther off from this dream than the blacks with whom they often share the same ghettos. Concentrated largely in the Southwest, Florida, and New York City, but living in all of the fifty states, Spanish-Americans display a growing political awareness and increasing militancy in their movement to gain equal opportunities with white Americans.

The term Spanish-American is used by the U.S. Census Bureau to label a mixed group of people who are vastly different from each other in their origins, their histories and culture, and their reasons for residence in the United States, but who share certain characteristics that identify them and unite them in their quest for a sympathetic audience. The Spanish-American population in the United States includes four groups according to the Census Bureau: Mexican-Americans, Puerto Ricans, Cubans, and a catchall group that includes any Spanish speaker not included in the first three. More than two thirds of the Spanish-Americans have Spanish as their native tongue, but they share other important characteristics as well. More than three fourths of the approximately ten million Spanish-Americans were born U.S. citizens, for instance. Nearly one fourth of them live near New York City or Los Angeles. To understand their surging energy and angry confrontation with the establishment, we should know that members of America's second biggest minority are young; their average age is twenty and a half compared with twenty eight for the general population of the U.S.

Half of the Spanish-Americans in the U.S. are of Mexican origin or descent, but what *Mexican-American* means is not always easy to define. Clearly the term includes those Americans of Mexican descent living in the Southwest who were residents of the land before the Anglos arrived. It no doubt includes the people from the steady migration from Mexico into the Southwest and the rest of the United States. It perhaps includes a reported 75,000 persons—mostly Mexicans—who have entered the U.S. illegally to live in southern California. But whatever the historical origins of the group, the newest defining characteristic of the Mexican-American is an increasing politicization and self-identification. From the militant Brown Berets in Southern California to such established political leaders as U.S. Senator Joseph M. Montoya of New Mexico, the chicanos—as the Mexican-Americans prefer to call themselves—show a visible bitterness and restlessness with their status in the American society.

Being Puerto Rican carries with it the dual condition of being a U.S. citizen and a Puerto Rican. For most, it means maintaining one's Spanish language and cultural heritage. For many, it means close home and family ties with the island of Puerto Rico. It means Puerto Rican customs, celebrations, food, movies, and religion. The situation for the individual attempting to be both American and Puerto Rican is made more difficult in the United States, say the activists, by racism which forces the Puerto Ricans to remain in the barrio and take the jobs no one else wants. Emerging political consciousness and know-how have, nevertheless, enabled such leaders as former Bronx Borough President Herman Badillo, now U.S. Congressman from the 21st District, to emerge— within the system—as a spokesman for many of his people. But the cultural pride of the militant youth makes them want to confront the problems as *machos;* in its extreme this results in the revolutionary Young Lords, who demand the right to run their own affairs without interference from the system.

Cubans living in the United States are joined to the other groups of Spanish-Americans by officialdom—the Census Bureau—because they have Spanish surnames. They share other characteristics as well which cause officials to take notice of them: most are recent immigrants to the U.S.; large numbers have remained in one location, Florida; and they present economic and education problems. But in a fundamental sense, Cubans in the U.S. remain in limbo. Many have not decided whether their destiny lies in the United States or whether it remains in Cuba. They are torn between joining the movements of other Spanish-Americans attempting to bring progress or joining efforts to return to a Cuba in which they would hold positions of power and responsibility.

More than one and a half million Spanish-Americans live in the New York City area, approximately one million in Los Angeles County, four hundred thousand in Miami. In spite of enormous gains made by individual Spanish-Americans in these areas during the past decade, millions more are embittered by their lack of progress and are beginning to make their frustrations felt throughout the United States. As a result, there is a closer relationship between the various Spanish groups, more ambitious self-help projects, greater local and federal government attention in an effort to bring new opportunity to Spanish-Americans. The only question is whether gains will be made through the active reformism advocated at present by most Spanish-Americans or through the violent revolution advocated by the most disenchanted.

9.1a What is the function of paragraph 1?

9.1b Which paragraph largely defines the term *Spanish-American?*

9.1c What are the four classifications of Spanish-Americans living in the U.S.? (In exercise 9.1j you will be asked to write about the fourth class.)

9.1d What method of development is used in paragraph 3?

9.1e What does the word *chicano* mean?

9.1f What is the meaning of the word *machos?*

9.1g Which paragraph defines Cubans? How does their problem differ from those of the Mexican-Americans and the Puerto Ricans?

9.1h Is the final paragraph an effective terminator for the theme? Why?

9.1i Read paragraphs 1 and 6 again (first and last). Can these two paragraphs stand alone as a theme? What information is included in paragraphs 2, 3, 4, and 5 that makes it a better theme?

9.1j Write a definition paragraph about the fourth class of Spanish-Americans mentioned in paragraph 2. Your paragraph should fit into the theme between the fifth and last paragraphs. It should begin with an appropriate transitional device to integrate it into the smooth development of the whole theme. You may wish to begin with a phrase such as "Nearly one fourth of the Spanish-Americans in the U.S. come from a number of different Spanish-speaking countries." You may include information about immigrants, students, professors, businessmen, and others from the Spanish-speaking regions of the Caribbean, Central America, and South America.

9.1(a) Name_____ Date_____

_____

_____

_____

_____

_____

_____

_____

_____

_____

_____

_____

_____

_____

_____

_____

_____

_____

_____

_____

_____

_____

_____

9.2 Write a theme of six or seven paragraphs in which you use the techniques of definition and classification. You may want to use the topics suggested in 7.8, 8.6, or any of the topics suggested in other lessons of the book that lend themselves to development through definition and classification.

Paragraph Development by Space and Time

10.1 The following paragraphs demonstrate the development of topics according to time sequences and space arrangements. In some instances, the subject may require the organization of ideas based on space or spatial relationships without reference to time. In discussing a contemporary topic such as the drug problem, you might write about events in New York City, Denver, Berkeley, and Kokomo with no specific reference to the dates of the events. Another subject may demand an organization based on the chronology of events with little or no reference to where the events took place. A political biography might stress a man's election to the U.S. Congress in 1933, his appointment to President Roosevelt's cabinet in 1942, a personal scandal in 1956, re-election in 1960, and so on, irrespective of the place in which these events occurred, either because the place is obvious or because it is not significant. Other subjects, major historical events for example, may require a method of development using both time and space relationships.

The first model paragraph demonstrates development through spatial relationships while telling a simple story of personal experience.

Recollections of the Grade School Principal's Office

"Young man, go to the principal's office!" were the most terrible words in all of grade school, usually spoken in near hysteria by one of a whole string of timid lady teachers. What brought terror to my heart wasn't the principal, but that office, the scene of a legendary, but nonetheless real, hell described so vividly by my five older brothers. As you walked in the office door, the first thing you noticed was the enormous desk about as big as our whole apartment. From my angle you could just see the principal's bald head and mean eyes looking at you over the top of the desk. Directly behind the desk was a window that the sun always seemed to be shining through, making you squint or look at the floor. Along the wall to the right of the desk was an old gray filing cabinet in which every misdeed was recorded in something called *permanent* records. If you ever got a chance to sit down, you sat on a cold plastic-covered couch that stood along the wall to the left of the desk. This always put you at a disadvantage because when you sat on that couch you couldn't even make your feet touch the floor. On the wall behind the principal's desk, on each side of the window, were large pictures of the graduating classes of the school. The only thing that made visits to the principal's office bearable was that while the principal told me what I couldn't do, I could look at those pictures and pick out the faces of my brothers grinning triumphantly.

10.1a What are the five objects described in the model paragraph of 10.1? What is the location of each object in relation to the other objects in the office? Which object provides the point of reference for the locations of most of the other objects?

10.1b Draw a simple floor plan showing the approximate locations of the objects mentioned in the paragraph. Label the objects in your plan.

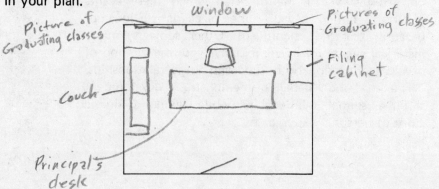

10.1c How does the terminator relate to the first two sentences?

Description from older brothers

10.2 The next paragraph demonstrates development through spatial relationships in a very small area. Try to visualize a painting of a mountain landscape as you read.

Looking at a Painting

A painting, among other things, is controlled or confined space, and our appreciation of a painting partially depends on how well we perceive the spatial relationships employed by the painter. To begin with, our vision is restricted or directed by the outer limits of the painting, a frame in most instances. We may perceive the painting as a "whole," but most often our eyes are directed by the painter to a focal point or center of interest. The focus of the picture alone would not hold our attention, however. We are led to it by the painter because of its significance through its relation to other objects in the painting. We might, for example, notice an outstanding face in the background in the midst of dark clothing and shadows. Or we see figures in the distance in the painting's perspective in contrast to a flat silhouette in the foreground that frames them. We are compelled to look at the clouds in the sky because our eyes are lifted upward by the lines of the trees or mountains in the painting. We observe that a large brown field in the lower left is balanced with a small, colorful cluster of trees on the right. In the end—in traditional or representational painting—we always return to the center of interest, which has been intensified for us by extending our sight to include the details visually supporting the main subject.

10.2a Before you attempt the following exercises, spend some time in looking at paintings and discussing with your classmates and teacher the artist's organization of spatial relationships.

10.2b What is the relationship between the main idea of sentence 2 (framing) and the main idea in the first part of sentence 1?

10.2c Some of the artist's techniques are only indirectly suggested in the paragraph. Which sentence indicates his use of color? Of perspective? Of light?

10.2d According to the paragraph, what effect does observation of the details of spatial organization in relation to the central focus have on the viewer?

10.2e All of the following words have rather special meanings in a discussion of painting. Check your dictionary to clarify the meanings of *spatial, perceive, focal point, focus, perspective, silhouette, representational.*

10.3 A short biography is best organized according to time. The important events of the person's life are listed within the paragraph. Observe in what order the dates of the events are given in the following paragraph.

Sequoya

He lived his mature years as George Guess, named after a white trader he believed to be his father. But it is his Indian name, Sequoya, that is perpetuated in the enormous evergreen trees of California in Sequoia National Park. Sequoya died in 1843, possibly near San Fernando, Mexico, in search of a group of his Cherokee tribesmen who had gone to the Far West, according to legend, before the Revolutionary War. His life as a famous teacher and scholar necessitated · many other journies, one of the most important in 1829 when he went to Washington, D.C., as representative of the western Cherokees. This trip was instrumental in reuniting the scattered Cherokees in the West, who had been forced from their eastern homes, into Indian Territory, now Oklahoma. He had himself gone west earlier to teach his alphabet for the Cherokee language to this fellow tribesmen. As early as 1828, the missionaries had adopted his alphabet—completed some years earlier—and had used it in printing the weekly paper *Cherokee Phoenix and Indian Advocate.* That was the same year Sequoya had gone on to Oklahoma from Arkansas. He had reached Arkansas in 1823, some years before the march westward by the Cherokees. It was in 1821 that the Cherokee Council approved his alphabet, the first writing system for the language. Actually, the system was a syllabary—a system using eighty-five characters standing for syllables to represent every sound in the Cherokee language. Although his people thought him crazy at the time, and his wife is said to have burned his birchbark notes, he is the only man known to have conceived and perfected a complete syllabary for a language. He had only begun the task in 1809. Very little is known of his life before that time, but he was a silversmith among the Cherokees in Georgia, having moved there some years after his birth in Taskigi, Tennessee, in about 1770. Sequoya, a Cherokee Indian whose name is honored through the giant Sequoia trees, was himself a giant among the American Indian peoples.

10.3a Is the first sentence in the model paragraph the topic sentence or is the last sentence?

10.3b What is the function of sentences 1 and 2?

10.3c Indicating the dates in the order given in the paragraph, list the major events of Sequoya's life in simple tabular form.

Sequoya's Life

Event	Year
Sequoya died	1843
Wash. D.C. as Cherokee rep.	1829
His alphabet adopted by missionaries	1828
Reached Arkansas	1823
Cherokee Council approved alphabet	1821
Began conceiving syllabary for language	1809
Born about	1770

10.3d The model paragraph is written in reverse chronology, which is a useful technique for achieving variety or emphasizing the events that are most recent. Natural chronology, of course, presents events in sequence, starting with those that occurred longest ago. It is generally easier to write a paragraph using natural chronological order. Taking the information in the model paragraph, rewrite the paragraph using natural chronology. Use the same, or nearly the same, topic sentence identified in 10.2a at the *beginning* of your paragraph. You may wish to select fewer than the eight dates and events given in the paragraph or add others from your own knowledge. You will need transitional devices appropriate to presenting material in natural chronological order.

Name _____ Date _____

_____

_____

_____

_____

_____

_____

_____

_____

_____

_____

_____

_____

_____

_____

_____

_____

_____

_____

10.4 Although dates are indicated in the following paragraph, they are not stressed. Notice as you read that the method of development, based on geographical space, stresses the movement and wide range of Alexander's conquests rather than what happened on what date in each place.

Alexander the Great

Whether moved simply by curiosity or by a thirst for conquest, one of the most fascinating and controversial figures in world history was Alexander the Great. From his first battle, the capture of Athens in 338 B.C., until his death thirty-two years later from a fever in Babylon, Alexander had personally led his armies across most of his known world. Like an enormous harvesting machine, Alexander and his armies moved from his home in Macedon south into Greece, across the sea to the lands east of the Mediterranean, and down into Egypt. Consuming the wealth and experiences of the East while, at the same time, spreading the language and culture of Greece, he crossed the ancient Persian Empire through central Asia on into India, his conquests including large portions of the three continents of Europe, Africa, and Asia. His empire was so vast, that on his death it was divided into five parts, each under the administration of one of his generals. Alexander is regarded in legend and history as both conqueror and hero, with mothers in central Asia naming their sons after him but using his name, when children misbehave, to instill fear in their hearts.

10.4a Which sentence first indicates that the paragraph is developed by space? What words or phrases accomplish this?

10.4b What words or phrases in sentence 4 relate to the concept of *harvesting machine* in sentence 3?

10.4c Is the final sentence an adequate terminator? Why?

10.4d Referring to the map below, discuss the conquests of Alexander in relation to the sequence of geographical areas mentioned in the model paragraph. The numbers on the map refer to locations mentioned in the paragraph. How does the organization of the material presented in the model paragraph reflect a logical spatial relationship?

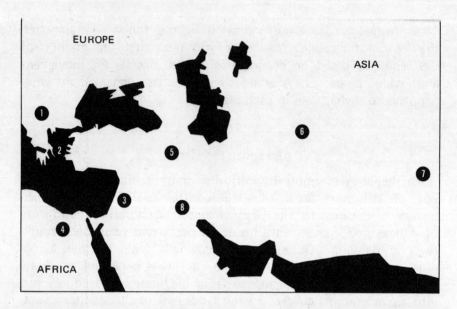

10.5 Read the following model paragraph, which discusses the conquests of a different group of people. This method of development based on natural chronology (time) and the countries where the conquests occurred (space) is frequently used in historical writing.

The Vikings

The Vikings invaded England in 793, eventually ruling all of it; their humble but vigorous and frank life style lives on in many of the words of the Vikings borrowed into the English language at that time. The daring exploits of the Vikings live on in the legends and myths of all Europe, for after England, they quickly and effectively sailed to other conquests. By 840, they had conquered all of northern Ireland. There were numerous assaults against France, but by 843, the Vikings were secure enough there to move out against Germany and the Low Countries. They were driven back from Spain in 859 but went on to conquests in North Africa during the same year and in Italy by 860. At the same time in eastern Europe, another group of Vikings had arrived on the Baltic coast of Russia in 860 and penetrated into the heart of the country, with little resistance. Their expansion westward was more peaceful if no less hazardous. The reasons for such a move are obscure, but by 930 approximately 20,000 people from the Vikings' homelands had settled in Iceland. In 985, the Vikings colonized Greenland. From there, in the year 1000, Leif Ericson led the Vikings on a journey that resulted in his discovery of America. Soon other populations became the forces of European destiny, but in a period of only two and a half centuries, the Vikings had come out of what we often regard as a dark, cold, mysterious Scandinavia to become the most fearsome naval power in Europe.

10.5a Where did the Vikings live originally?
10.5b Underline the topic sentence in this paragraph.
10.5c Rewrite the final sentence so that it could serve as a topic sentence at the beginning of the model paragraph.

The Vikings ventured from Scandinavia, their homeland to invade England in 793.

10.5d The conquests of the Vikings covered three large geographical regions according to the paragraph: eastward toward Russia, westward toward Iceland and Greenland, southward throughout Europe. In what sequence are these geographical areas developed?

10.6 Read the following model paragraph. Notice that the paragraph is developed by the use of both time and space.

Grape Cultivation

The history of grape cultivation is as old as the history of man. Fossilized grape leaves, stems, and seeds have been taken from Tertiary deposits of perhaps 30,000,000 years ago. In man's

Basic information from *Encyclopaedia Brittanica*. Chicago: William Benton, Publisher, 1963.

recorded history, we have details of grape and wine production depicted in mosaics of the Egyptians of 2400 B.C. It is theorized that cultivation of the grape originated in the area around the Caspian Sea and from there grape growing spread to Asia Minor and Greece. In Homer's time, about 1000 B.C., wine was a common feature of Greek life. From Greece, grape culture spread to Sicily. The Phoenicians carried the grape to France as early as 600 B.C. Pliny, writing before A.D. 100, described ninety-one varieties of grapes and fifty kinds of wine. The Romans planted grapes along the Rhine River in Germany by A.D. 200 and probably took them to England as well. Columbus and later the colonists of the seventeenth and eighteenth centuries brought the European grape to America, where it achieved its present-day success only after it was crossed with the disease-resistant, native, wild American varieties.

10.6a Which sentence first indicates that the paragraph includes information based on space?
10.6b Learn the following words: *fossilized, Tertiary, mosaics, theorized.*
10.6c In a simple tabular form, list in the blanks on the next page all places with corresponding dates mentioned either directly or indirectly in the paragraph. Notice there are more places than dates mentioned. Even though both time and space are useful methods of development in this paragraph, they do not receive equal emphasis.
10.6d Read the following paragraph and compare it with your chart in 10.6c.

One theory is that cultivation of the grape originated in the area around the Caspian Sea. From there grape growing spread to neighboring areas of Asia Minor, then to Greece, and from Greece to Sicily. The Phoenicians carried the grape into France, and the Romans planted grapes in Germany and England. As grape cultivation spread into the West, grapes were moved into the East by way of India. Everywhere that new lands were settled, people took the grape along. Columbus and later colonists brought the European grape to America, where it had little success until it was crossed with the native American varieties.

1. What is the method of development, time or space?
2. What kind of information in your table in 10.6c is largely omitted in the developmental technique in paragraph 10.6d?

Grape Cultivation

Place	Year
Originated around Caspian Sea	
Spread to Asia Minor and Greece	
Greece to Sicily	
Phoenicians carried grape to France	600 B.C.
Romans, Rhine River in Germany	
+ probably England	A.D. 200
Columbus to America	
Colonists in America	17TH + 18TH cent.

10.6e Read the following paragraph and compare it with your table in 10.6c.

The history of the grape is as old as man, and older. In fact, fossilized grape leaves, stems, and seeds have been taken from Tertiary deposits of perhaps 30,000,000 years ago. But in man's recorded history, we have details of grape and wine production depicted in mosaics of 2400 B.C. during the Fourth Dynasty of Egypt. In Homer's time, about 1000 B.C., wine was a common feature of Greek life. By 600 B.C., grapes were carried to France, and no later than A.D. 200 they were introduced into Germany. The writer Pliny, before A.D. 100, described ninety-one varieties of grapes and fifty kinds of wine. Columbus and later the colonists brought European grapes to America, were they found native varieties already growing in a wild state.

1. What is the method of development?
2. What kind of information in your table in 10.6c is largely omitted in the developmental technique in the paragraph in 10.6e?

10.6f Which of the three paragraphs about the cultivation of grapes (10.6, 10.6d, 10.6e) do you feel is most successful? Why?

10.7 A paragraph developed by space is an attempt to create in words a visual sense of an area. It cannot duplicate what one could actually see if he were on the spot, but, nevertheless, it has certain advantages. It can indicate a point of view, direct your reader's attention, and restrict his vision in a certain direction or in a special sequence. In a paragraph describing your campus, you might develop the paragraph by space in several different ways:

1. You might use some important landmark, for example the Student Union Building, and describe other locations in relation to it. The order in which you discuss each location is not as important as its relationship to the landmark.

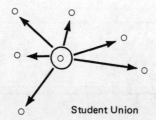

Student Union

2. You might use an important landmark as the starting point and move from it to the next location, on to another, and so on, perhaps ending back at the original landmark.

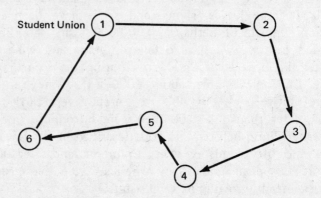

3. Another type of development by space might stress the boundaries of an area. The order in which these are listed is not necessarily important.

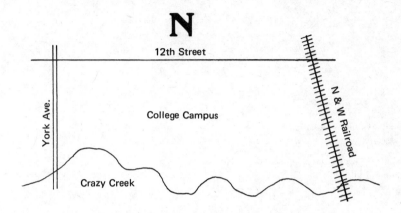

4. Still another spatial development might stress the inter-relationships between locations. The order is not necessarily important.

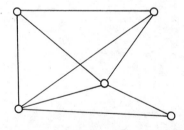

Write two paragraphs developed by space. Use one of the methods just described for the first paragraph, and one of the other three methods for the second paragraph. Try to visualize the spatial organization before you write. A diagram or drawing might help you organize your ideas more clearly. Possible writing topics might include:

Exploits or conquests of a historical figure
Migration or movement of a group of people
Description of the arrangement of a room (a house, a city, a geographical area)
Dissemination over a geographical area of a discovery (a religion, a food, an idea, a social practice)

10.7(a) Name _____ Date _____

10.7(b)   Name_____   Date_____

10.8 A paragraph developed by time is often like a list paragraph, a natural chronology providing the order in which the list of events is given. Paragraph 10.3 provided a model for a reverse chronology; other model paragraphs used a natural chronology. Still other organizations of time can be employed in writing. Some fiction, and often contemporary movies, alternate from present to past to future with little regard for natural chronological order. Since this method of development is more difficult and is used infrequently in academic prose, it has not been given any attention in your text.

Write a paragraph developed by time. Use a natural chronological order for the events you select. Possible writing topics might include:

Important events of the day (week, month, year, decade)
Development of an industry (an institution, a state, a sport, a
   movement or cause)
Biography or autobiography

10.8(a) Name _____ Date _____

_____

_____

_____

_____

_____

_____

_____

_____

_____

_____

_____

_____

_____

_____

_____

_____

_____

_____

_____

Paragraph Development by Process Description

11

11.1 Process description is very similar to a recipe; it follows definite steps in a necessary order. Keep this comparison in mind as you read the model paragraph.

Water Purification

The provision of safe water results in one of the major expenditures of manpower and revenue in our modern cities. The purification of water is basically a two- or three-step process carried out under the strict supervision of public health scientists and engineers. As the first step, natural water from the least contaminated source is allowed to stand in large reservoirs where most of the mud, clay, and silt settle out; this is called "sedimentation." Often in water with high mud content, lime and aluminum sulfate are added to the water in the settling reservoirs. These chemicals react in the water to form aluminum hydroxide, which settles slowly and carries much of the suspended material, including most of the bacteria, to the bottom of the reservoirs. As the second step, the water is filtered through beds of sand and gravel, removing still other impurities and chemicals in the

131

water. During or after filtration, antibiotic chemicals are ordinarily added to the water to kill any remaining harmful bacteria. Chlorine is one of the most common chemicals used for this purpose. A third step taken by some municipalities is adding to the water other beneficial chemicals such as fluoride to make tooth enamel hard and soda ash to make the water itself soft. The water purification process, carried out with little variation from one large city to another, is perhaps the biggest factor in the prevention of major outbreaks of disease in this century.

11.1a What is the function of sentence 1? If you had read only sentence 1 and stopped, without knowing the content of the rest of the paragraph, what are several different ways of continuing the paragraph? If this were a simple list paragraph, you might proceed as follows:

> The provision of safe water results in one of the major expenditures . . .
> Another major expenditure is allocated to the maintenance of good roads . . .

11.1b What is the function of sentence 2? How does this sentence rule out most of the possibilities for continuing the paragraph discussed in 11.1a? What key words in the sentence determine the content and development procedure of the paragraph?

11.1c Sentences 3, 6, and 9 introduce the different steps in the water-purification process. What function do the intervening sentences serve that distinguishes the process paragraph from the simple list paragraph?

11.1d What words or phrases in the terminator relate it to the topic sentence?

11.1e In the model paragraphs of lessons 1 and 2, the points or examples used as developers have no necessary order or sequence. With very slight changes of transitional devices, points or examples might be presented in a very different order with no essential change of meaning in the paragraph as a whole. Can the same be said of the process paragraph? Why?

11.2 The organization of the following paragraph is somewhat different from most of the models in this book. It does, however, have all of the requirements of a good paragraph including a topic sentence.

Making Wine

The first essential in the production of a good wine is a good grape harvest. In Europe, grapes are usually harvested when they are at their sweetest in September and October. Some varieties of grapes are picked one by one, while others are picked in bunches with the stems remaining on even during the pressing stage of production. The methods of pressing, by means of which the juice is extracted, vary from place to place, but stamping or treading on the grapes is still popular in some wine regions. The most important step in the wine-making process, however, is fermentation. When the must (the pressed grapes and juice) stands, the yeasts from the grape skins release enzymes that change the grape sugar to ethyl alcohol and carbon dioxide. This action raises the alcoholic content from between seven to fourteen per cent and produces other substances that give wines their characteristic flavors. Both the oxygen supply and the temperature must be carefully controlled during fermentation; otherwise vinegar bacteria might take over and convert the alcohol to acetic acid. When fermentation has ended, the wine is put into wooden casks, leaving the skins and residue behind. After standing for a period of time, it is drawn off to other casks, each time clarifying and leaving the sediment behind. This step is usually repeated several times until the wine is judged ready for bottling. Making wine is a complex process involving the several steps of harvesting the grapes, extracting the juice, fermenting the juice, refining the wine, and caring for the wine until it is bottled. Variation in any one of the steps can influence the quality of the final product.

11.2a In most of the paragraphs you have studied, the topic sentence has appeared at or near the beginning of the paragraph. Which sentence in this paragraph is the topic sentence?
11.2b The three steps in the process of water purification described in 11.1 are clearly marked by obvious enumerative phrases. How many distinct steps are described in the process of making wine? What are the enumerative or transitional phrases that move the reader from one step in the process to another?
11.2c Is each step of a process described or elaborated by a fixed

Basic information taken from *Collier's Encyclopedia*. New York: The Crowell-Collier Publishing Company, 1965.

number of sentences? What determines the amount of explanatory material presented in connection with a given step?

11.2d Since the topic sentence comes near the end of the paragraph, it serves the double function of *stating* and *summarizing* the main ideas of the paragraph. The last sentence in the paragraph also has a double function. One of these is that of terminator, bringing the paragraph to a psychologically satisfying conclusion. What do you think the other function is? Relate your answer to the distinction between a list paragraph and a process paragraph.

11.3 The following paragraph is quoted from *Industrial Sociology.* It is presented here—admittedly out of context—simply as an excellent example of process description from a widely used textbook.

There are certain similarities in the histories of minority groups in American industry. First, a demand is created for labor, either by the location of a factory within the living area of a minority group or by the creation or expansion of industry in another place. Second, the members of the minority group are attracted to the industry because of the higher wages which can be earned there, of the excitement of working in the city, or of the lack of existing economic opportunity. Third, the minority group members enter the factory at the bottom level, filling the unskilled roles, performing the hard "mean," dirty jobs. Their entrance is bitterly opposed by the earlier arrivals. Fourth, a struggle develops between earlier arrivals who hold the better positions in the factory—who are skilled workers and foremen—and the new arrivals who quickly begin to strive for the better things they see about them. This struggle sometimes involves physical violence. More often it is fought out by discriminating against the new arrivals. The ranks of the entrenched groups are closed to the new arrivals. Mythologies are created respecting the superiority of the entrenched group and the natural ineptitude of the new group. Derogatory names are applied to the out-group. Fifth, the new minority breaks through the walls erected by the entrenched older workers, perhaps in a crisis such as might be brought on by a war, perhaps through

Eugene V. Schneider. *Industrial Sociology: The Social Relations of Industry and the Community.* Second Edition. New York: McGraw-Hill Book Company, Inc., 1969, pages 464-465.

superior energy. The newly successful group then consolidates the ground it has won; it sees to it that only compatriots are hired or promoted. It reserves the best jobs for itself. Sixth, the cycle begins over again with the arrival of a new group.

11.3a In this well-constructed process description, the topic sentence (sentence 1) establishes the context of the process developed in succeeding sentences. The last sentence in the paragraph is a very effective terminator. Discuss this sentence in terms of the definition of a restatement given in 2.1a. How is the word *cycle* effectively used in its psychological function as terminator?

11.3b Learn to spell and use the following words, which do *not* appear in the passage you have just read. In the space opposite each word, write a word from the passage that has approximately the same meaning.

pejorative　　　　　　　　　＿＿＿＿＿＿＿＿＿＿＿＿

menial　　　　　　　　　　＿＿＿＿＿＿＿＿＿＿＿＿

technician　　　　　　　　＿＿＿＿＿＿＿＿＿＿＿＿

incompetence　　　　　　　＿＿＿＿＿＿＿＿＿＿＿＿

"brothers," "compadres"　　＿＿＿＿＿＿＿＿＿＿＿＿

legends　　　　　　　　　　＿＿＿＿＿＿＿＿＿＿＿＿

11.3c Discuss with your classmates and teacher the validity of the author's analysis of the integration of minority groups into American industry as well as the details of the process.

11.4 The eight sentences below, which are printed in a scrambled sequence, if rearranged would constitute a process-description paragraph. In the spaces at the left, put the numbers of the sentences in the sequence in which they would occur in a well-ordered paragraph. When the sentences are properly arranged, they constitute a paragraph with the following structure:

Introduction
  Two topic introducers and a topic sentence
Body
  Four developers describing four steps of a process
Conclusion
  One terminator

The Americanization of Asia

____   Thus, the flow of people and goods and the expansion of world communication have caused at least the superficial aspects of American life to become universally familiar, even if not universally adopted.

____   This Americanization of Asia proceeded as a four-step process of U.S. expansionism.

____   Initially, the process grew out of economic and political considerations—the need for a sluggish economy to find new markets and the cold-war ideological competition with the communist countries.

____   Americans like to export their ideas along with their products.

____   Especially in Asia during the 1950's and 1960's, American ideology and technology spread from Turkey to Taiwan, from Afghanistan to Ceylon.

____   The sending of American technicians and experts to the target country, which often occurred concurrently with the first three steps, provided Asians with new life-style models.

____   Massive military aid supplied to a given target country enabled the country to resist the counterinfluence of Russia and China.

____   Economic, educational, and technological aid extended the infrastructure and know-how of the target country, leading to the rise of an independent spirit as well as an expanding economy.

11.4a Discuss with your teacher and your classmates your reasons for arranging the sentences in the sequence you determined.

11.4b Give reasons for arranging the developers (the steps in the process) in the sequence you used.

11.4c Read the sentences in the arrangement you have established in order to experience the paragraph as a unified whole.

11.4d The meaning of a word is more than its dictionary definition. Discuss the meanings of the following words as they are used in the paragraph. Do you have any emotional responses to the words or ideas they convey?

  ideology,   ideological,   expansionism,   target   country,   infra-structure

11.5 One method of defining terms or describing a process is by analogy, that is, pointing out how two things which seem quite unlike are similar in some respects. The following paragraph develops only half of an analogy between cooking and writing.

Writing is a little like cooking. The mental processes you go through in the preparation for writing are similar to the mechanical steps in the preparation of a hearty soup, for example. First, there must be a compelling hunger that motivates you to begin such a difficult task. Once a decision is made to get on with the job, the ingredients must be collected, the correct proportions determined, the order of combining the ingredients decided upon, and the most appropriate container selected. Next the mixture is put on a low fire where it simmers and boils for a period of time, changing the nature of the mixture through the amount of heat used and the length of time cooked. Finally, the aroma of the food and the energy expended in cooking it force you to sit down and eat, as you give the soup the undivided attention it deserves. The process is not necessarily complete though, for eating may suggest changes in the recipe—less pepper, more water, fewer carrots—changes to be carried out at another time that would result in an improved version of the product.

11.5a Sentence 1, the topic sentence of the paragraph, compares writing to cooking. Then follows a description of the several steps involved in preparing a hearty soup. In brief phrases, describe the corresponding steps in writing a paragraph or theme.

Cooking	Writing
compelling hunger that motivates	
ingredients must be collected	
order of combining parts	
simmers and boils	
eating	
changes in the recipe	

11.5b What other steps not listed above do you feel are important in the writing process?

11.5c In the space provided at the beginning of the model paragraph, supply an appropriate title.

11.6 The following paragraph also discusses an aspect of the writing process. Think of this paragraph in relation to the model paragraph of 11.5.

Editing

Getting your thoughts down on paper is not the final stage of writing a good paragraph, even though it may result in a tremendous weight being lifted from your mind. Editing is the process that finally shapes your ideas into an acceptable and highly individual paper. Think of the editing process in terms of the changes you make between sentences, within sentences, and in individual words in your first draft of the paragraph. At the word level, spelling and capitalization are checked, but more creatively, words are often changed; a different word may be substituted for the original word because it is easier to understand, is more colorful, gives a more precise meaning, provides variety. At the sentence level, phrases may be put in a different order, structures of modification revised, different verb structures selected, the length of the sentence and phrases altered. These editorial changes add polish and maturity to your writing. Finally, for smoothness and balance, changes are made between the sentences, clarifying relationships and providing better coordination between ideas by punctuating more adequately, by choosing better transitional devices, and by adding or taking out phrases. Editing, the self-conscious appraisal and revision of your own writing, makes the difference between a poor writer whose ideas are not communicated to his reader and a good writer whose ideas have the maximum effect on the reader.

11.6a Which sentence in the model paragraph defines editing?

11.6b The process description in this paragraph—editing—is organized around what three elements?

11.6c What transitional devices are used to introduce the development of each element?

11.6d How does the terminator refer back to the definition of editing given in sentences 1 and 2 of the paragraph?

11.6e The easiest way to understand the editing process is to read two earlier versions of a paragraph that you have already studied in 11.4.

1. This is an early draft of the paragraph that was satisfactory in its overall organization. It included topic introducers, a topic sentence, three developers (steps in the process), and a terminator.

The Americanization of Asia

Americans like to export their democracy along with their automobiles. Since the second world war and the comfortable national prosperity of the 1950's and 1960's, countries in Asia have increasingly come under the influence of American ideology and technology. This Americanization of Asia, from Turkey to

Taiwan, is actually a three-step process brought on by the cold war ideological competition with the Communist countries and the need for an expanding economy to develop new markets for its produce. One step includes massive military and economic aid to enable the target country to resist the counter influence from Russia and China. Another step involves educational and technical aid to extend the knowhow of the target country in achieving an independent spirit as well as an independent economy. The third step, which may occur concurrently with the first two, consists of increased trade with the target country, which results in expanding their markets but also in extending our products and markets. The increased flow of people and goods, and increasing world communication has resulted in at least the superficial characteristics of American life becoming universally recognized if not universally followed.

2. Even though the paragraph organization was adequate, the paragraph could be improved by editing. The following is the edited version. Read the paragraph line by line. Which changes represent editing at the word level? The sentence level? Between sentences?

The Americanization of Asia

Americans like to export their ~~democracy~~ *ideas* along with their ~~automobiles~~ *products*. Since ~~the second world war~~ *World War II* and the comfortable ~~national~~ *U.S.* prosperity of the 1950's and 1960's, ~~countries in Asia~~

~~have increasingly come under the influence of~~ American ideology *have increasingly influenced countries in Asia.* and technology, This Americanization of Asia, from Turkey to

Taiwan, is actually a three-step process. brought on by the cold-war ideological competition with the Communist countries, and the need for an expanding economy to develop new markets for its produce, *and by* ~~One step includes~~ massive military and economic aid ~~to~~ enables the target country to resist the counter‿influence

from Russia and China. ~~Another step involves~~ <u>e</u>ducational and

technical aid ~~to~~ extend<u>s</u> the know‸how of the target country in

achieving an independent spirit as well as an independent economy.

~~The third step~~, (which may occur concurrently with the first two*steps,*)

~~consists of~~ increased trade with the target country,~~which~~ results in

developing
~~expanding their~~ markets‸ ~~but also in extending our products and~~
                                                              for both countries.

                                                                    expanding
~~markets~~. The ~~increased~~ flow of people and goods, and ~~increasing~~

                    have made
world communication‚ ~~has resulted in~~ at least the superficial

                            become   *familiar even*
characteristics of American life ~~becoming~~ universally ~~recognized~~ if

    adopted.
not ~~universally followed~~.

3. The edited version, without editorial marks, appears below.

The Americanization of Asia

Americans like to export their ideas along with their products. Since World II and the comfortable U.S. prosperity of the 1950's and 1960's, American ideology and technology have increasingly influenced countries in Asia. This Americanization of Asia, from Turkey to Taiwan, brought on by the need for an expanding economy to develop new markets for its produce and by the cold-war ideological competition with the communist countries, is actually a three-step process. Massive military and economic aid enables the target country to resist the counterinfluence from Russia and China. Educational and technical aid extends the know-how of the target country in achieving an independent spirit as well as an independent economy. Increased trade with the target country, which may occur concurrently with the first two steps, results in developing markets for both countries. The flow of people and goods, and expanding world communication, have made at least the superficial characteristics of American life become universally familiar, even if not universally adopted.

4. Compare the version of the paragraph in (3) above with model paragraph 11.4 which follows. Notice that paragraph 11.4, a still later version, incorporates other changes, including an additional step in the process.

The Americanization of Asia

Americans like to export their ideas along with their products. Especially in Asia during the 1950's and 1960's, American ideology and technology spread from Turkey to Taiwan, from Afghanistan to Ceylon. This Americanization of Asia proceeded as a four-step process of U.S. expansionism. Initially, the process grew out of economic and political considerations—the need for a sluggish economy to find new markets and the cold-war ideological competition with the communist countries. Massive military aid supplied to a given target country enabled the country to resist the counterinfluence of Russia and China. Economic, educational, and technological aid extended the infrastructure and know-how of the target country, leading to the rise of an independent spirit as well as an expanding economy. The sending of American technicians and experts to the target country, which often occurred concurrently with the first three steps, provided Asians with new life-style models. Thus, the flow of people and goods and the expansion of world communication have made at least the superficial aspects of American life become universally familiar, even if not universally adopted.

11.7 Write a process-description paragraph employing the techniques illustrated in this lesson. Write the first draft of your paragraph on the next page. After a period of time, perhaps a day, write an edited final version of your paragraph on the following page. The following topics may help you get started.

Preparing a speech (a lesson, a demonstration)
Teaching someone to swim (skate, ski, drive, cook)
The modernization of neighborhoods (schools, laws)

11.7(a) Name_____Date_____

First Draft

_____

_____

_____

_____

_____

_____

_____

_____

_____

_____

_____

_____

_____

_____

_____

_____

_____

_____

_____

_____

11.7(b) Name_____ Date_____

Final Version

_____

Theme Development by Time, Space, and Process

12.1 In lesson 9 you studied a theme that employed two methods of development. The following incomplete theme combines the techniques of definition, time, space, and process to discuss a contemporary labor movement. The complexity of the various elements and influences making up the subject matter requires a combination of developmental techniques. After you read the theme once, reread each paragraph carefully to determine the method of development used. You will be expected to complete the theme later.

La Causa

_____ For more than three years, until the middle of 1970, a California grape strike and boycott captured the attention of the American public as no other agricultural strike had ever done. When it reached its peak, it had gained the support of the store owners and shoppers of the

nation and had become *La Causa* for the
Mexican-American community. With eighty
per cent of the Mexican-American population
living in the cities, *La Causa* was more than a
grape pickers' strike; it was the first dramatic
advance of the Mexican-Americans, urban and
rural, to a visible position in American society.

_____ *La Causa* has been described as a union, a
nonviolent civil-rights movement, and a self-
help association. But it started in California as
a strike to gain representation for chicanos,
equality under the labor laws, and basic
human rights and dignities. It has continued
to fight for other agricultural workers such as
the seasonal pineapple industry laborers in
Hawaii, but more especially the migrant
workers who follow the crops from Florida to
Michigan, Texas to Montana. Only in the
months after the grape strike ended did *La
Causa* enter the public consciousness as a
term characterizing the Mexican-American's
struggle in the U.S. against discriminatory
wage practices and inequitable educational
opportunities—poverty and ignorance.

_____ *La Causa* is led by Cesar Chavez, whom
Time magazine described at the time of the
strike as "...a onetime grape-picker who
combines a mystical mein with peasant earthi-
ness." Born in 1928 in Arizona of mixed
Spanish and Indian blood, Chavez reached his
eminence as the most prominent Mexican-
American leader through years of appren-
ticeship to poverty and prejudice. During the
Depression his family became migrants, pick-
ing, hoeing, weeding, digging, or pruning its
way up and down California, the seasonal
crops dictating their next move. Chavez went

to thirty different schools even though he never got past the seventh grade and had to teach himself to read and write. For more than ten years, he worked with the Community Service Organization on voter registration and citizenship programs, and as a labor organizer, but in 1962 with his wife and family in Delano, California, he began the long preparation for the grape strike. Forming the National Farm Workers' Association, Chavez's first dramatic victory was a three-hundred-mile march from Delano to Sacramento, which started with seventy-five workers and ended with eight thousand farm workers and city friends; one large wine-producer agreed to negotiate before the march ended. But Chavez had table-grape growers as his target. Mounting a massive boycott that stretches from California across the U.S. and even to England and Scandinavia, Chavez forced nearly all the table-grape growers to sign contracts by the fall of 1970. The boycott was ended, but not *La Causa.*

To understand the real power of Chavez, one must see how *La Causa* became not only a strike against working conditions among the grape-pickers but a symbol of the aspirations of Mexican-Americans to gain a full role in the U.S. society. Chavez first started the National Farm Workers' Association on $1,200 of his own savings. By means of personal contact with the workers through 300,000 miles of travel in California, Chavez enrolled one thousand members in the union by 1964. He provided incentive and unity to members through death-benefits, a credit union, and a newspaper. When Chavez felt it had gained enough strength, the union sued a company for paying less than minimum wages and won. The next step, organized by Chavez, was a strike by a group of workers against a grower who finally gave a 120% wage increase. After the successful march to Sacramento, Chavez decided on the boycott. Public opinion grew in support of Chavez until, just before the harvest in 1970, all but a few of the growers had signed contracts with the AFL-CIO United Farm Workers Organizing Committee. Chavez's success with the strike and boycott elevated him to sainthood in the Mexican-American community, where *La Causa* was seen no longer as a grape strike but the cause of all chicanos in America's future. . . .

12.1a Label each paragraph in the model theme using the term studied so far to describe methods of development and structural function studied so far. For example, topic paragraph, restatement paragraph; or process, time, space, classification, definition, comparison, contrast, and so on.

12.1b Which paragraph defines *La Causa?*

12.1c List some of the qualities or characteristics that help define

La Causa. _____

_____

_____

12.1d In paragraph 3, would you say time is more important as a method of development, or space? Why?

12.1e What is the significance of the biography of Chavez in paragraph 3 in relation to the movement *La Causa?*

12.1f In the space provided on the next two pages, write a paragraph that satisfactorily concludes the account of *La Causa.* The content of your paragraph should bring the account up to date, indicating what has happened since 1970. The method of development for the paragraph should employ the techniques of time and space. In addition, the paragraph should be an effective terminator for the theme. Reread the entire theme when you have finished writing.

12.2 Using the techniques first described in 7.6, with your classmates and teacher select a topic that can suitably be developed through time, space, and process. Develop an oral composition with the class. Choose a topic of your own, or refer to 10.8 and 11.7 for other possible topics for an oral composition, or you might wish to discuss one of the following:

Non-European contributions to American culture (music, art)
The spread of English as a world language

12.3 Write a theme of five to eight paragraphs in which you use the techniques of space, time, process, and any other method of development discussed in this book. The theme should convey an overall sense of movement through time or space or a progression through the steps of a process description. Individual paragraphs may support this overall development by definition, classification, comparison, and so on. Avoid mixing too many methods of development, however, for the theme may then lack focus. You may want to use a topic of your own choice, or one of the topics suggested in 10.8 and 11.7, or any of the topics mentioned in other lessons of the book that lend themselves to development through space, time, and process.

Paragraph Development by Cause and Effect

13.1 The stating of facts and the giving of reasons to explain why or how the facts came about is the basic procedure of paragraph development by cause and effect. Observe the procedure as you read the following paragraph.

Slaughter on the Highways

During the past five years, the number of Americans killed annually in automobile accidents has climbed to more than 55,000. This needless slaughter on our streets and highways can be attributed to three general causes. Mechanical failures, especially those related to faulty brakes and bald tires, account for a significant number of fatal accidents. Environmental conditions such as blind corners, narrow streets, heavy fog, intermittent rain or snow resulting in slippery pavement also contribute to the grisly accident statistics. But without doubt the most frequently reported factors in automobile accidents are errors of human judgment—all the way from such follies as excessive speed and drunken driving to such momentary lapses as failure to signal a turn or a change from one lane to another. The man behind the wheel is often his own worst enemy.

13.1a In which sentences do you find the causes in this paragraph?

13.1b In which sentence do you find the effect?

13.1c What is the function of sentence 2?

13.1d The last sentence in the paragraph neither states a cause nor an effect. What is its function?

13.2 The following fragment has the basic structure of a cause and effect paragraph. Read it and plan an appropriate completion of the causal relationships suggested in the last sentence.

Causes of Student Failure

Thirty-six per cent of the entering freshmen at a large midwestern university are dismissed during or at the end of the first year. Studies indicate that this alarming rate of failure is due to a variety of causes, some of which are beyond the control of the student. Among these are inadequate academic and personal counseling services, inferior quality of instruction in very large freshman sections, and the computerized anonymity of most administrative procedures. But many of the causes of early student failure can be traced to nonadaptive behavior on the part of the

student himself. _____

_____

_____

_____

_____

_____

_____

13.2a In the space provided, write three sentences that give reasons for student failure in the first year of college. Remember that these reasons must be factors within the students' control.

13.2b Write an appropriate terminator for this paragraph.

13.2c Which sentences in the paragraph state the causes? Which state the effect?

13.2d What is the function of sentences 2 and 4?

13.3 The next model paragraph demonstrates a rather straightforward development, listing four causes of environmental pollution.

Environmental Pollution

It isn't yet clear whether man will choke in his own smog or smother in his own garbage. Refuse and waste—the by-products of a gluttonous, overproductive, consumer economy—pollute the air, contaminate the water, and desecrate the land. Our large industries belch foul gasses into the air and vomit deadly chemicals into the rivers and oceans. The phallic automobile rapes the virgin countryside with an insatiable lust for new thoroughfares and freeways and emits noxious fumes into the cities' anoxic air. But it is the astronomical increase in population over the past seventy-five years—devouring the natural resources, including space, and defiling the already imbalanced environment with waste—which is the greatest contributor to pollution. Whatever the causes of our environmental ills, and these are just a few, it is clear that unless strong remedies are taken, the patient will most certainly die.

13.3a What is the function of sentence 1? Do you feel it is effective? Why?

13.3b The four causes of pollution mentioned in the model paragraph are not introduced by such repetitious introductory phrases as "one cause is . . . another cause is . . . ." Can you list each cause in a few words?

_____

_____

_____

13.3c The effect—environmental pollution—is not directly stated in the terminator. How does the sentence refer to the effect?

13.3d How does the terminator refer back to sentence 1?

13.3e How are you supposed to feel about pollution after reading this paragraph? What words in the paragraph are especially effective in making you feel this way?

13.4 The technique of cause and effect has great flexibility, for the relationships between causes and effects are not always as clear-cut as the two terms seem to suggest. Causes may not all carry the same weight, for example. Several causes may be grouped together to form one important cause. There may be one effect to a cause, or there may be many. Effects may be less important than causes. And so on. The next few model paragraphs, selected from textbooks, further demonstrate cause and effect in the kind of academic writing you are likely to read. They show considerable variety in their methods of indicating the relationships between causes and effects. Because the paragraphs are taken out of context, the method of paragraph development may seem less obvious; as you learned in the model themes, one paragraph in a longer paper builds on the previous paragraphs and anticipates the next. Exercises are therefore kept to a minimum, discussing only the most obvious features of the paragraphs.

Several factors cause fatigue, but in general, they come down to two main causes: lack of fuel or food, and the excessive accumulation of by-products of activity. Muscle activity uses up stores of glycogen or sugar. It also must have oxygen, for a muscle deprived of it will soon cease to contract. Lactic acid and carbon dioxide are the chief by-products of muscle activity, but there are also toxins from other sources which may help produce fatigue. Some of these toxins may come from bodily infections and some may be absorbed from breathing or from the digestive process. But in addition to these factors, there are certain causes of fatigue which are more or less obscure. Some of these are less physiological than psychological, such as lack of interest in what you are doing. When you do something that bores you, you tire easily; if you are interested in your work, you forget the amount of energy you put into it. You also tire more quickly when standing than when you are walking, for in walking, each leg rests half of the time.

Cleveland P. Hickman. *Health for College Students.* Second Edition. Englewood Cliffs, New Jersey: Prentice-Hall, 1963, page 126.

13.4a The topic sentence indicates there are two main causes of fatigue. Which sentence indicates that still other causes are going to be discussed?

13.4b Does the paragraph have an effective terminator?

13.4c Reread sentence 1 in the model paragraph of 13.4. Write a topic sentence on pollution, using the pattern of sentence 1, 13.4. Substitute your own wording appropriate to pollution and its causes based on the information in model paragraph 13.3.

_____

_____

_____

13.4d Would you have the same reaction to a paragraph about pollution developed from this new topic sentence as you did to 13.3? Why?

13.4e Although this paragraph is clearly organized, it also seems to suffer from fatigue. Can you explain why the paragraph seems tired?

13.5 The following model paragraph is taken out of context from *Society and Thought in Modern America.* You are at some disadvantage because you do not know what came before this paragraph, and the effect is not stated until the final sentence. In addition, the causes do not really seem to be causes until you read the last sentence, at which time the relationship is clearer. Read the paragraph at least two times before attempting the exercises.

Nineteenth-century America, devoted to the doctrine of *laissez faire,* fell behind Canada and other large immigrant-receiving countries in providing supervision over the arrivals who in so many cases had left ancestral villages of a backward technological level. Despite this failure to direct the immigrant, old settlers denounced the unbearably congested cities where the immigrants crowded together for understanding and mutual aid in segregated Little Italys, Little Hungarys, Polonias, and Ghettos. Trade unions, ever fearful of economic competition, doubted whether these unskilled workers would ever be more than strikebreakers and a depressing

Harvey Wish. *Society and Thought in Modern America.* New York: Longmans, Green and Company, 1952, pages 238-239. By permission of David McKay Company, Inc.

influence upon wages and living conditions. Still another irritant was racialism. By the end of the century European racialist theories, encouraged by the advance of nationalism, had acquired the prestige of "science," and had penetrated reputable eastern American colleges. The dogmas of Anglo-Saxon superiority and the survival of the fittest were invoked to classify those of the New Immigration as biologically and morally inferior to the "Aryan" races. Restrictionists had already stopped most of the Chinese immigration on similar economic and racial grounds. The next such movement produced the restrictionist laws of 1917, 1921, and 1924. The end of the traditional hospitality of the United States toward immigration was in sight.

13.5a *Why* questions very often state an effect and call for answers that are causes. For example, one way of discussing the subject matter of this paragraph is to ask yourself the question: Why was the end of traditional hospitality toward immigration in sight? Your answer would be a list of the causes. How many causes can you identify?

13.5b *Doctrine of laissez faire, immigrant-receiving, strikebreakers, depressing influence upon wages, racialist,* and *restrictionists* are examples of jargon in writing. *Jargon* is the specialized vocabulary of people in the same work or field of study. What is the hazard of using jargon in writing about a subject?

13.5c Is the final sentence an adequate terminator? Is it a restatement?

13.6 The method of development in the following paragraph demonstrates another variation of the cause-and-effect relationship. Read the paragraph carefully.

There has been an emphasis, recently, on the possibility that society itself, or the group culture, may be producing the distortions of personality, mental illness, and emotional instability which apparently are widespread. Various writers have pointed out that man's basic needs are being extensively thwarted by the demands of society. According to this view, man no longer may be an individual or develop his imagination, reason, and creative

Louis P. Thorpe. *The Psychology of Mental Health.* Second Edition. New York: The Ronald Press Company, 1960, page 18.

powers; and he is prevented, because of society's compartmentalizing, from achieving feelings of relatedness—of loving and being loved. Because of the competitive demands of civilization, man now strives for "things" rather than for his own development. He feels himself to be merely a pawn rather than a contributing member of his society. If he rebels, he is subject to punishment by society, or if, on the other hand, he submits, he may become simply a stereotyped, pedestrian member of society and thus lose much of his urge toward creativity and individuality. As an example, Fromm suggests that society produces in its members what he calls "a socially patterned defect."[1]

[1] Erick Fromm, *The Sane Society* (New York: Rinehart and Company, Inc., 1955), pages 15-21.

13.6a In which sentence is the cause-and-effect relationship first indicated? Is it the topic sentence?
13.6b Explain how the phrase "socially patterned defect" summarizes the whole paragraph and refers back to the topic sentence.

13.7 The subject of the following paragraph, the growth of the labor force in the nineteenth century, is not specifically mentioned until near the end of the paragraph. Does it seem to be a cause or an effect?

With the beginning of the factory system, labor needs could be met in part by long working hours. In an economy where agriculture prevailed, it was not unusual that factory operators should insist upon sunup to sundown as a normal working day. Factory labor was at first recruited from the women and children in the towns and villages surrounding the factory areas. The first persons employed in the Slater mills, for example, were seven boys and two girls between the ages of seven and twelve. In the Massachusetts mills, the general policy was to employ female operatives who were boarded at company houses and subjected to considerable company control insofar as conduct was concerned. Such employments, significant as they might have been, were a "drop in the bucket" in terms of labor requirements. The

Sanford Cohen. *Labor in the United States.* Second Edition. Columbus, Ohio: Charles E. Merrill Books, Inc., 1966, page 11.

explanation of labor force growth in the nineteenth century is closely related to the history of the population growth that occurred. An important element in the population growth was the tide of immigrants who came to the United States in increasing numbers until government policy discouraged large-scale immigration after the first world war.

13.7a List the three causes for the growth of the labor force discussed in the model paragraph.

_____

_____

_____

13.7b Do the three causes seem to receive equal emphasis?
13.7c What is the function of sentence 6?

13.8 Cause and effect is an extremely advantageous developmental technique for use in longer papers. In lesson 3, we discussed black performers in television by the technique of examples. This subject could be enlarged upon by a discussion of the causes for the increased demand for black performers. The model paragraph in 4.5 discussed the migration of Southern blacks and Puerto Ricans to New York City. This subject could also be given greater scope by indicating causes for the migration.

As you have seen in the model paragraphs in lesson 13, cause and effect can be used in developing individual paragraphs on a variety of subjects. This technique is appropriate for subject matter ranging from the trivial "Why I Hate Breakfast" to more serious topics such as "The Causes for the Re-emergence of Venereal Disease as a Major Health Problem."

Write two cause-and-effect paragraphs on any two of the following topics or others of your own choice: major causes of adolescent rebellion (or crime, or drug use among the young, or pollution in my city, or smaller and smaller candy bars, or the rise and fall of skirt lengths).

13.8(a)   Name _____ Date _____

13.8(b) Name _____ Date _____

_____

_____

_____

_____

_____

_____

_____

_____

_____

_____

_____

_____

_____

_____

_____

_____

_____

_____

_____

_____

Paragraph Development by Generalization

14.1 Paragraph development by generalization is very much like paragraph development by examples (see lesson 2). Both make use of developers, which are examples supporting an idea or point of view. One common difference is that the generalization is stated as a *conclusion* based on several examples, given as facts or opinions, which *lead* the reader to make the same conclusion. The focus of the reader's attention is on the generalization. It is less like telling the reader "This is true because of this and this and this" and more like saying "If this is true, and this and this, then we can make the following *general conclusion*, can't we?"

The Decline of Small Businesses

Each year, countless small businesses close their doors and go into bankruptcy. The corner grocer, the little dress shop, the locally owned sandwich shop, the baker, the dance studio and club, the beauty salon, all are victims of the constantly shifting economy. They are, at times, replaced by other small businesses that temporarily fill the needs of the neighborhood but frequently end up sharing the same fate of dissolution. More often, the market served by the small business is taken over by a large store or plant, frequently from a more distant place of operation. Typically the corner grocer's and baker's business has already gone to the nationally owned supermarket down the street. The sandwich shop is replaced by a hamburger shop, one of a large chain, or a franchised food shop specializing in chicken, fish, or pizza. The woman who runs the dress shop chooses fashions out of tune with the times and gets too old to keep the store open during the most convenient hours for shoppers, who then go off to the big department stores. It is increasingly difficult, apparently, for small businesses to succeed in our complex economic structure based, as it is, on small profit margins and tremendous sales volume.

14.1a What is the function of sentence 1?
14.1b Sentence 1 is a statement of observable fact that could be supported with statistics from cities and states throughout the country. Compare sentence 1 with the final sentence. How do they differ? What factors are stated in the generalization that do not appear in sentence 1?
14.1c What kind of information do the developers provide that leads to the generalizations?
14.1d Point out words or phrases in sentences 2 through 6 that lead you to accept the generalization, especially the final phrase of the generalization: " . . . complex economic structure based, as it is, on small profit margins and tremendous sales volume."

14.2 The following incomplete paragraph leads you to make your own generalization. On the basis of the casual examples given in the paragraph and other observations of your own, what would you conclude about *news?*

Nightly News

Turn on the news broadcast any evening, and the predominant mood is one of gloom. Maybe Brazil and Peru didn't go to war, but the news is that Jordan and Israel did. At least four movie stars are reported to be heading toward divorce, but nobody reports that several million couples got through the day without a single fight. On the way to school or work in any major city, thousands of men and women ride in close proximity exchanging pleasantries, or at least civilized silence, without making the news, but the rapist in the park provides the major story on the final

report._____

_____

_____

_____

_____

_____

14.2a Notice that each developer includes one item of what might be considered good news and one item of bad news. In the space provided, add one more sentence that contrasts bad news and good news.

14.2b Which news—good or bad—dominates the presentation of news items in the paragraph and in newscasts generally?

14.2c Complete the paragraph with an appropriate generalization. Since the generalization in this paragraph, as in 14.1, comes at the end, remember that it should also be an effective terminator.

14.2d What words or phrases in your final sentence refer back to sentence 1?

14.3 Paragraph development by generalization is employed for a variety of reasons. It may be used to gently persuade and lead the reader to the writer's point of view. It may establish rapport by stating a conclusion that is rather obvious and already agreeable to both reader and writer. It may point out a foregone conclusion or generalization upon which the writer wishes to build additional information and opinions. For these purposes, and others as well, authors of the type of material you will be reading in your academic course work often use generalizations. The following model paragraphs are excerpts from popular textbooks in such subjects as English language, geography, and sociology. They exemplify a wide variety of generalizations, and as in lesson 13, exercises are kept to a minimum.

The surface of the earth is chiefly water—something that we, as dwellers on the land, are apt to ignore or completely forget. As noted earlier, the Pacific Ocean alone covers nearly one third of the globe. The combined areas of all water bodies, including oceans, seas, and lakes, add up to nearly two and one-half times that of all the land of the earth. In other words, about 71 per cent of the earth's surface is water. In addition to the large expanses just mentioned, there are small ponds, waters that run as streams on top of the land, and other waters that lie or move within the upper portion of the earth's crust. And there is water in vapor and condensed forms in the atmosphere. Thus, water is an important and practically all-pervasive element in man's habitat.

14.3a Which sentence states the generalization in this model paragraph?
14.3b The structure of this paragraph is very similar to the model paragraph in 14.1. Sentence 1 begins with a statement of observable fact. Compare sentence 1 with the final sentence. How do the two sentences differ? How is the relationship between the two indicated?

14.4 The following paragraph contains three related generalizations. As you read the paragraph, try to discover the way in which these generalizations are interrelated.

When most of us think about language, we think first about words. Thus, the hardest part of learning a foreign language may seem to be memorizing its vocabulary; when we observe a child first acquiring speech, we talk of his progress as a matter of learning new words. We are also likely to feel that the adult speaker with the largest vocabulary has the best command of English. To think of a language as just a stock of words is, however, quite wrong. Words alone do not make a language; a grammar is needed to combine them in some intelligible way. Moreover, words are relatively easy to learn, and indeed all of us go on learning them all our lives. They are also the least stable part

Henry W. Kendall, Robert M. Glendinning, and Clifford H. MacFadden. *Introduction to Physical Geography.* New York: Harcourt Brace Jovanovich, Inc., 1967, page 59.

Thomas Pyles and John Algeo. *English: An Introduction to Language.* New York: Harcourt Brace Jovanovich, Inc., 1970, page 96.

of language. Words come into being, change their pronunciations and meanings, and disappear completely—all with comparative ease. Yet it is true that the vocabulary is the focus of language. It is in words that sounds and meanings interlock to allow us to communicate with one another, and it is words that we arrange together to make sentences, conversations, and discourse of all kinds. Thus we have a paradox in that the most ephemeral part of language is also the center where meaning, pronunciation, and grammar come together.

14.4a Which sentence states the first generalization?
14.4b Which sentence provides a transition from the first generalization toward the second?
14.4c Which sentence states the second generalization?
14.4d In what way does the third generalization make use of the first two?
14.4e This paragraph exemplifies a very persuasive technique using generalizations. Notice that the first generalization, which, as the authors indicate, everyone believes, is stated initially so that the authors can knock it down later with a second generalization. The second states a different point of view although it is still incomplete. The authors are able, in the final sentence, to pull the different ideas expressed in the first two generalizations into a defensible third statement that clearly represents the authors' views. As you can observe in the paragraph, it is an interesting and effective technique to lead you to a modified point of view or a new understanding of the subject.

14.5 The following model appears at first to be paragraph development by example. The topic sentence provides you with a statement that can be supported by facts or examples. It is followed by several historical examples. Observe closely, however, the effect of the paragraph's final two sentences, which include the quotation from Frederick Douglass, writing in the nineteenth century as an ex-slave.

In the context of city life slaves lived under fewer restraints than in the countryside. In theory, slaves were not allowed on the city

August Meier and Elliott M. Rudwick. *From Plantation to Ghetto.* New York: Hill and Wang, 1966, pages 65-66. By permission of the publisher.

streets without passes from their masters. In practice, however, it was difficult to confine slaves to their quarters in their masters' courtyards; it was inconvenient to prepare passes every time a servant was sent on an errand about the town. Therefore, the urban slaves had considerable freedom in coming and going, simply because it was easier for their masters. Moreover, a number of slaves, especially those hiring their own time, were permitted to live out. Their wooden shanties, ordinarily in the alleys of the commercial areas and on the edge of town, were inferior physically to the quarters in the master's yard, but the added degree of freedom was highly prized. Indeed, though the number of urban slaves declined, the number of those living out rose. Also prized was the right to worship in Negro churches, which were usually mixed congregations of free people and slaves. Even some prominent white ministers defended the practice of permitting separate religious institutions for Negroes. All of these things allowed much informal socializing, not infrequently in illicit dramshops run by white saloonkeeprs. Although the public feared that such gatherings were seedbeds of revolt and crime, attempts to circumscribe this sort of activity largely failed. "A city slave is almost a free citizen," declared Frederick Douglass, with pardonable exaggeration, when he compared his experiences in Baltimore during the 1830's with his earlier life on Maryland's Eastern Shore. "He enjoys privileges altogether unknown to the whip-driven slave on the plantation."

14.5a In what way does Douglass' statement generalize beyond the facts stated in sentence 1?

14.5b What words or phrases in the last two sentences in the paragraph refer back to sentence 1?

14.5c What is the function of the sentence beginning "Although the public feared such gatherings . . . "

14.6 Generalizations, as we have pointed out in this lesson, are based on several examples or instances that lead the writer and reader to form a conclusion. You could write a generalization based on only one example, but the conclusion would be less convincing unless it were already self-evident or some universal truth. The sentence containing the generalization may appear at the beginning or the end of a paragraph, but in the planning stage you normally think of the generalization first. Then you develop the examples that can effectively lead up to the generalization. Remember that the main purpose of the generalization paragraph is to convince the reader that your conclusion is the only logical one.

Write two generalization paragraphs on two different topics selected from the following or on other topics of your choice.

Social or economic problems of blacks (Spanish-Americans, Indians, rural whites, or other minority groups)
Life in the '70's (the twentieth century, the city)
On being twenty (young, old)
Woman's role (in the '70's, in marriage)

14.6(a)   Name _____   Date _____

14.6(b)   Name _____ Date _____

Theme Development by Various Means

15

The three samples of expository writing presented in this lesson were all written for purposes other than inclusion in a composition text. Nevertheless, they are included here because they contain good examples of the organizational techniques *from paragraph to theme* illustrated throughout this book.

15.1 The following is the first paragraph of a speech delivered by Herman Hudson on September 11, 1970, before the faculty of Indiana State University in Terre Haute, Indiana. As you read the paragraph, try to anticipate the organizational plan of the whole speech.

Blacks and Black Studies in a Predominantly White Society

The most urgent socio-political problem that America faces now and in the decade ahead is the question of how to bring about rapid and substantial improvement in the quality of life of her black citizens. As citizens, black Americans justly demand for themselves equal enjoyment of the rights of citizenship on a par with white Americans. Black people claim the right to obtain a good education which includes the truth and dignity of the black experience. Black people claim the right to full employment in jobs consistent with their training and experience. Black people claim the right to live in decent housing in attractive surroundings. Black people claim the right to have control over the police and judicial procedures that vitally affect their lives. In most American communities, South and North, black people are consciously and systematically denied these basic rights. I believe the denial of these rights is immoral; the continued denial of these rights is impossible. The problem is urgent and its solution imperative, preferably by rational planning rather than by irrational confrontation.

15.1a The first and last sentences of the paragraph are the topic sentence and the restatement, respectively. The first sentence states the general theme of the paragraph and the speech as a whole. The last sentence restates this general theme but with greater structural compactness and rhetorical tension. How is this accomplished? In answering, it may be useful to look at the three segments of the restatement separately in relation to ideas expressed or suggested in other sentences of the paragraph: The problem is urgent / and its solution imperative / preferably by rational planning rather than by irrational confrontation.

15.1b In the body of the complete speech, how many distinct developmental sections would you expect to find on the basis of your reading of the opening paragraph? In short phrases, indicate the probable content of these developmental sections. (Recall the procedure of theme development illustrated in lessons 3 and 6.)

_____

_____

_____

_____

15.1c Sentences 3, 4, 5, and 6, which introduce specific points to be developed later, all begin with the same words. There are no connectors or transitional devices between these sentences. What do you think is the speaker's intention in presenting a series of developers in this way?

15.1d What are your opinions of the claims of black people to the rights mentioned in the paragraph? Which one of the claims might be considered controversial? Why do you think the speaker placed this claim in the position it occupies in the list?

15.2 The following excerpt from the speech deals with education or more specifically with Black Studies programs. Read through the entire passage concentrating on both its form and its content. Then work through the exercises at the end. Numbers have been placed beside each paragraph to serve as reference points for class discussion.

Blacks and Black Studies in a Predominantly White Society

(1) Now let us turn our attention to the place of Black Studies programs in schools and colleges. The college student revolt of the 1960's shocked the conscience of the nation. No longer was it possible to ignore the brutalizing effect of injustice, racism, and war. Young militants broke the bonds of traditional patterns of thinking and launched a devastating attack on the hypocrisy and immorality of many of our social institutions. Some, fortunately a minority, found the disfunction and dehumanization of our society so intolerable that they simply dropped out. Most critics, however, thrust forward a variety of demands calculated to cure the ills that so sorely afflict the nation. Universal among these remedies in the field of education was the demand for the establishment of Black Studies programs.

(2) In response to the exigencies of the moment and with little regard for the long-term academic and budgetary consequences, hundreds of Black Studies programs have been set up in all sections of the country, in all kinds of institutions, from the small private college to the multiple-campus state university. Gradually, over the past two years both students and educators have begun seriously to grapple with the issues involved in defining the objectives, the sphere of operation, the curriculum, and the academic justification for such programs. Questions such as the following have been raised and debated, and in many institutions they remain unresolved today. What are the vocational implications of a major in Black Studies? Who should be the students and who should be the teachers in these programs? Why have a separate Black Studies program at all when the relevant courses are already

available or could be easily introduced in the traditional departments of our colleges and universities?

(3) For me, many of these questions can be answered very
simply. Inasmuch as both black and white students have been
victims of the fraudulent treatment of the black man's role in the
development of America, both groups, though for different
objectives, need the corrective of Black Studies courses. As for the
teachers in a Black Studies program, ideally they should be black.
However, with the rapid proliferation of such programs and the
interim scarcity of black professors, white professors may be used
so long as it is clear to one and all that blacks are in control of the
program.

(4) The obvious rationale for the establishment of independent
Black Studies departments is the fact that the traditional departments of our colleges and universities historically have promoted
the distortion of the black man's role in American society and,
therefore, they are hardly qualified to set the record straight.
Structurally, the Black Studies program should be an autonomous
department with a regularly established independent budget co-
equal with other departments in the College of Arts and Sciences.
Its faculty members should have the same rights and responsibilities as other faculty members, and they should have wide scope
and administrative encouragement to devise innovative research and
instructional activities. Only as an independent department, the
fundamental academic unit of colleges and universities, can the
Black Studies program have the stability and permanence necessary
to its unique educational mission.

(5) As for those who inquire how can you make a living with a
major in Black Studies, I refer them to the many and varied
occupations besides teaching, outlined in such articles as "The
Black Studies Graduate in the 'Real World' " by W. Smith, for
which a Black Studies major provides an excellent preparation.[1]
Moreover, a growing number of institutions now allow a double
major instead of the older undergraduate pattern of a major and a
minor. More extensive curricular adjustments, including greater
flexibility in setting distributional requirements for graduation, are
gradually being introduced. Such reforms greatly facilitate the
design of undergraduate programs with both an occupational and

[1] William D. Smith, "The Black Studies Graduate in the 'Real World,' " *Personnel and Guidance Journal*, 48 (May, 1970), 767-768.

cultural focus. In my opinion, a forced opposition between Black Studies as a major and an established work-oriented field, such as engineering for example, is really a false issue. One can easily have both in any modern university addressing itself to the contemporary needs of its students. But the whole question of the vocational utility of Black Studies is quite irrelevant to the group necessity that blacks feel to have such programs.

(6) What are the most frequently stated purposes or objectives of Black Studies programs? After examining some forty Black Studies proposals and programs in a great variety of institutions, Charles Hamilton of Columbia University, in a recent article entitled "The Challenge of Black Studies," summarizes the following six:

1. *The Gaps Function.* Many proposals list courses in the humanities and in social sciences and history whose descriptions state that the courses are aimed at correcting the inadequacies of existing courses. They tend to fill the "gaps." They emphasize contributions of black people, etc.

2. *The Functional Theory.* This defines those proposals that say their major purpose is to educate black students for useful service in the black community once they have graduated. Usually, the emphasis here is on community organization stressing courses in black economics, black politics, and the like. At times, a proposal will suggest that the Black Studies program could be a useful pre-law or pre-medical or pre-architectural program, or at least an undergraduate major in preparation for subsequent professional training in a traditional field.

3. *The Humanizing Function.* Here the target is white students who will take courses that will help overcome white racist attitudes by imparting new knowledge and hopefully, thereby, new human values.

4. *The Reconciliation Theory.* Black Studies, some proposals state, will bring about a new spirit of cooperation between blacks and whites. This is an extension of function 3.

5. *The Psychological Function.* Black Studies will instill a sense of pride in black students, who will study and learn about their heritage and history. They will develop a sense of identity.

6. *The Ideological Function.* Some proposals clearly state that the overall function is to serve as means to develop new

ideological, Third World orientations, to develop theories of revolution and nation-building . . . [2]

(7) Each of the above purposes and objectives alone constitutes a legitimate rationale for black studies, and various combinations of them are implicit to one degree or another in many of the newly established programs. But the most important function of black studies programs, in my view, is to politicize people of color by means of a psychological conversion to blackness. By a psychological conversion to blackness, I do not mean merely the wearing of a tiki, an Afro, or a dashiki, for these are external badges which may or may not symbolize internal commitment. Nor do I mean that true blackness is necessarily revealed by incorporating in one's speech the hip jargon of radicalism, for this too may be feigned rather than felt. Nor is the spirit of blackness a newly invented thing by today's college generation, who after all learned about soul food, gospel, the blues, sacrifice, and survival from their parents who in turn learned these things from their parents.

(8) The conversion to blackness that I advocate is rooted in the inner faith that the destiny of all Afro-Americans is indivisible, that the survival of the group is more important than the progress of the individual, that the addict shooting dope in the ghetto is just as much a brother as the bourgeois suburbanite. No single black person can be truly secure before the law, on his job, in his home, or in the nation's schools and colleges until the masses of black people are liberated and secure. To be black then is to derive strength and self-confidence from identification with the suffering and the success, the pain and the poverty, the gains and the glory of a shared black heritage.

(9) Recently, in a seminar discussion on the role of Black Studies in educating the miseducated held at Indiana University, the lecturer asked a militant student, "Sister, are you black?" The student answered, "I think I am." "But how do you know?" the lecturer questioned. The student unhesitatingly responded, "I feel it in my bones." This was precisely the right answer, for the Negro who does not feel it in his bones just isn't black and he can never release his full psychic power for self-realization that alone can

[2] Charles V. Hamilton, "The Challenge of Black Studies," *Social Policy*, 1, No. 2 (1970), 16.

make him a whole man. This liberation of psychic energy through the joy of black identity, I suspect, is what people are describing when they refer to a feeling of "soul." Well-designed Black Studies programs controlled by blacks, I believe, can help cultivate this feeling.

(10) Incidentally, I do not mean to suggest that all Negro college students will want to major in Black Studies. Some will aspire to careers in education, or medicine, or business, or professional athletics. Others may prefer the newer fields of electronics or computer technology. Still others will prepare themselves for the new opportunities in such traditional areas as home economics, social work, or the allied health sciences. It is only to be expected that, since the minds, talents, and motivations of Negro youth vary greatly, they will make different occupational choices in accord with individual interests. But the one transcendent choice that all Negroes have to deal with at one stage of life or another is the choice of ethnic identification, and the satisfactory resolution of the question of self image is the necessary prerequisite for success in any endeavor. I am convinced that the most powerful regenerative force for black survival is a black man defining himself emotionally, intellectually, and ethically in terms of his black brothers and sisters. As a recent paraphrase of an old saying puts it: "What does it profiteth a dude to gain the world if he loses thereby his soul brother."

(11) In addition to the psychological function, Black Studies can provide the factual base and the analytical techniques that will enable future black leaders to reinterpret the black man's role in American society, in the past and present, and to project realistic strategies to improve his condition in the years ahead. Whatever the black man's role in America is to be, it will be a changing one as the whole society moves in new directions, and it will be a role in which the black man takes increasing responsibility for its formulation and design. Black Studies can provide the setting for the development of a sense of black heritage and the exploration of black destiny.

(12) A well-designed Black Studies curriculum should have at the core carefully articulated courses in Afro-American history, literature, music, and art. There should also exist on the part of the Black Studies faculty a specific commitment to develop new and

creative courses in such areas as the black theater, the black novel, the history of the education of black Americans, and the big city ghetto and independent black communities. Such courses should have both an academic and social action orientation. The relative emphasis on academics or social action will be conditioned by the location and resources of each institution.

(13) Let me conclude by restating what I believe to be the challenge and the opportunity before us as we prepare ourselves to prepare our students for an uncertain future. Black people today are uncompromisingly insisting on their right to participate in those decision-making processes that vitally affect their lives—all the way from national housing and education policies, to the control of local police, to the semantics of self-designation. The term *black*, once a pejorative epithet as used by whites, has been converted into a symbol of ethnic pride because colored people, or Negroes, decided for themselves that "black is beautiful." Black people want to choose their own leaders and spokesmen, define their own socio-economic goals, design the reconstruction of their own neighborhoods, recover and preserve their own cultural identity. Our schools and colleges through generous and sustained support of imaginative Black Studies programs can help prepare black people to achieve these goals. All that is needed is the will to do so.

15.2a Sentence 1 of paragraph (1) provides a transition from preceding sections of the speech and also states the main subject matter of paragraphs (1) through (12). The body of paragraph (1) is developed chronologically in broad strokes leading up to the widespread establishment of Black Studies programs. Why do you think that dates are largely omitted in the paragraph?

15.2b The two-part phrase at the beginning of paragraph (2)—In response to the exigencies of the moment / and with little regard for the long-term academic and budgetary consequences—might conceivably be placed elsewhere in the sentence. Why is it probably more effective where it is? What does the second part do?

15.2c The asking of questions for which a speaker believes he already has good answers is a very common device in oral discourse. Notice that paragraph (2) contains a number of questions answered in succeeding paragraphs. Are these answers presented in the same order in which the questions are raised? What determines the order and length of the answers?

15.2d Which questions does paragraph (3) answer?

15.2e Which question does paragraph (4) answer?

15.2f Which paragraphs respond to the questions regarding the practical and psychological usefulness of Black Studies within the black community?

15.2g Which issues raised in paragraph (2) are commented on in paragraph (12)?

15.2h Assuming the inclusion of sections of the speech not given in the excerpt but anticipated in 15.1 and 15.1b, discuss paragraph (13) as a restatement paragraph and summary of the whole speech.

15.2i In the spaces below, write the phrases or sentences from 15.1 that relate the subject matter to that found in the restatement paragraph.

1. Black people today are uncompromisingly insisting on their rights . . .

_____

_____

2. . . . the control of local police . . .

_____

_____

3. . . . define their own socio-economic goals . . .

_____

_____

4. . . . design the reconstruction of their own neighborhoods . . .

_____

_____

5. Black people want to . . . recover and preserve their own cultural identity.

_____

_____

Cite other correspondences in subject matter between the two paragraphs.

_____

_____

_____

_____

15.2j Viewed from the perspective of the speech as a whole, paragraph 15.1 and 15.2 (13) are the topic paragraph and the restatement paragraph respectively. Viewed from the perspective of the individual paragraphs, what technique of internal paragraph development is used?

15.2k Which two paragraphs together constitute a negative-positive definition sequence?

15.2l Which paragraph is an example of a simple list paragraph?

15.3 "*Easy Rider* and Its Critics" is a controversial critique of a 1969-70 award-winning movie. It also is an excellent model of the type of organization that is extremely effective in writing reviews or book reports. As you read the selection, keep in mind the following points. (1) The analysis of the movie does *not* begin with a summary of the story. Rather it begins with a statement of the author's thesis that art or drama has the power of moral and social instruction. (2) This thesis becomes the context in which the ethical message of the movie is discussed. (3) The résumé of the plot is shaped by and subordinate to the author's view of the purpose of serious theater. (4) The author includes a discussion of the critical opinions of other reviewers as well as a statement of her own judgment of the movie. (5) The last two paragraphs of the review reaffirm the moral influence of art and the moralizing function of critics.

Easy Rider and Its Critics

Bernard Shaw's *Quintessence of Ibsenism* was first presented in 1892 as a lecture to the Fabian Society in London. Shaw's

Diana Trilling, "*Easy Rider* and Its Critics," *The Atlantic*, 226 (September, 1970), pages 90-95. Reprinted by permission of the author, who holds the copyright.

justification for bringing the theater into discussion with people chiefly engaged in government, politics, economics, and the law was his belief that the drama has a significant influence upon the individual life and the life of society. "Art," Shaw wrote, but he was speaking primarily of the theater, "should refine our sense of character and conduct, of justice and sympathy, greatly heightening our self-knowledge, self-control, precision of action, and considerateness, and making us intolerant of baseness, cruelty, injustice, and intellectual superficiality and vulgarity." A formulation like this was possible eighty years ago as it of course no longer is; today, its language must seem to verge on quaintness. We nevertheless recognize that Shaw is voicing a conviction which in transmuted form is still very much alive for us. Certainly it is some such appreciation of the high moral function of the theater that warrants our appeals for government support of the stage and makes the basis of our contempt for the philistine and commercial theater.

And his statement of the high purpose of the dramatic art makes plain why Shaw found it appropriate to talk about Ibsen to a group of people whose first commitment was to political and social improvement. For if it is the purpose of the theater to instruct us in character and conscience, then clearly all men of character and conscience, all persons devoted to the public good, should be informed of the way in which the theater is discharging, or might discharge, this important duty.

There can be no question that were Shaw addressing himself to present-day affairs he would put the film under quite as strict scrutiny as the stage, or even stricter, and not merely because the movies reach so much wider an audience than stage plays but also because he would be bound to respond to the special force of the visual as compared to the predominantly verbal medium. Indeed, I have only a most formal hesitation in borrowing his authority for the opinion that no art now exerts more moral influence than the films, and that for the present generation, and particularly among our best-educated young people, more than personal character is being formed by our film-makers: a culture, a society, even a polity.

It is as an exemplification of this power of moral and social instruction that I wish to discuss *Easy Rider*. But perhaps I should first say what I mean by instruction in this context. I do not mean overt pedagogy, and I do not even mean what the famous director Jean-Luc Godard presumably had in mind when he was speaking at Harvard recently about his film *See You at Mao,* and said, "The movie is like a blackboard. A revolutionary movie can show how the arms struggle may be done." *Easy Rider* is not at all a film of this order. Although it is highly tendentious, it wears the mask of disengagement; its atmosphere, in fact, is that of a pastoral. Its method is that of implication and suggestion rather than that of assertion. Its notable achievement lies in its ability to communicate states of feeling: it is through its skill in the creation of emotion and mood that it does its work of persuasion.

An air of purposive mystification, a sense of the existence of tensions which are perhaps made the more significant by never being named, is established from the start of the film. *Easy Rider* opens with its two main characters, Wyatt, played by Peter Fonda, and Billy, played by Dennis Hopper, having crossed the border from California into Mexico to do business with a Mexican peasant. Both the young men are long-haired, one of them bearded, and both wear clothes which, like their style of hair, at once authenticate their dedication to freedom. Both are riding simple motorbikes. It is of some importance, I think, that Fonda and Hopper are the leading actors in a film which they wrote together, with some unspecified assistance from Terry Southern, and which Hopper directed. *Easy Rider* represents an unusually direct statement on the part of its authors: there are no paid "stars" to intervene between them and us, no interposition of an alien personality or will.

The business on which Wyatt and Billy have crossed to Mexico is the purchase of heroin. At least, we conclude it is heroin although it could of course be cocaine—it is a white powder and the two men sniff it. Apparently the purchase is satisfactory, because they then go on to their next rendezvous: a chauffeur-driven Rolls-Royce meets them at what seems to be the edge of an airfield, and a sallow and sleazy man of about forty—we notice that he is close-shaven and wears city clothes—gets out and takes their supply of drugs, in exchange for which he gives Wyatt and Billy a wad of money which they will later stash away in their bikes. Before this unalluring character drives off and out of the film, he takes his own revitalizing snort of the powder he has purchased. Although he is doing precisely what the two young men had done just a moment before, his use of the heroin is made to seem ugly and furtive whereas theirs has been presented as an exercise in connoiseurship—apparently with dope as with sex it is the style of the agent which makes for the moral meaning of the act.

As a first gain from the sale of the heroin, the simple motorbikes on which Wyatt and Billy were riding at the start of the picture are replaced by a pair of the biggest, flashiest, most expensive motorcycles ever to fill the male American heart with envy. It is on these splendid vehicles—Fonda-Wyatt's is decorated with a splash of American flag—that the two men now begin their beautiful journey from California to near New Orleans, where their trip will be suddenly and violently cut off. It is a handsome travelogue, this West to East tour of the Southwestern United States. And we are no doubt the more moved by the loveliness and variety of the country because it is offered to us as the stage on which two people already certified as heroes of dissidence are about to act out their fate. Too, this is an America whose purity has not been polluted. The landscape of *Easy Rider* would seem to have known no human desecration other than the building of the highways which Wyatt and Billy ride—they pass no cars, no buses, no billboards or roadside stands or motels. When there is any form of human encounter, which is rare, it is played for its symbolic meaning.

Thus, the two young riders stop at a lone ranch for repairs on one of the motorcycles. The rancher is shoeing a horse, and in his barn the wheel on which the camera fixes its editorializing gaze is that of a wagon. But even the farm itself is something of an anomaly in Fonda and Hopper's vision of the American West: we have been shown no other such instances of human enterprise. And indeed, the rancher inhabits a boundless universe; the land is his as far as the eye can see—what the film appears to be asking us is why, in an America this big and empty, we crowd as we do in our cities. He receives the two strangers at his table and within his family in the kind of openness and trust which consorts with the freedom and openness of the life he lives. His wife serves him in sweet docility, surrounds him with the happy-faced children she breeds for him. In a brief colloquy over their meal—in the idyllic imagination of *Easy Rider* farmers eat their meals at picnic tables set outdoors—Wyatt inquires whether all this vast spread belongs to the farmer, and he receives his host's assurance that it does. It is a good life to live, is Fonda-Wyatt's comment, and it is of course our response as well.

A counterpoint to this scene is provided very little later in the film when Wyatt and Billy, once again on the road, pick up a traveler—his style is not unlike their own—who takes them to his rural commune. Until now, *Easy Rider* has engaged in considerable conscious evasion: it has not told us where its two main characters come from or where they are going, what drug they have trafficked in or what use they plan to make of the money they earned by its sale, or, for that matter, what in their previous personal or social experience has brought them to their present condition. But now the film becomes not so much mystifying as surrealist. The commune contains some thirty or more young people and a few small children who all live together in what is no doubt meant to represent an entire goodness and harmony, each pursuing his concern. Playacting appears to be one of the group occupations: we see bits of miming in the manner of the guerrilla theater and even a rude outdoor stage. There is also a prayer scene similar to the Thanksgiving devotions in *Alice's Restaurant;* I took it, perhaps wrongly, to be an appeal for rain to water the crops—for it is a gentle point of this commune sequence that these young people would wish to grow their food but do not know how, their unnatural modern upbringings having cut them off from the vital springs of life: dazed but intent, they stamp barefoot upon the unharrowed, even unplowed, ground on which they have dropped the seed. Drugs are not mentioned; for one viewer, they were nevertheless omnipresent in the appearance and behavior of the members of the commune. There is a moment when the camera circles the group, moving slowly from one vacant-eyed face to the next: they are the faces of madness, of a perhaps irremediable break with reality, or so they looked to me, but I am afraid that what I saw was not necessarily what the makers of the film intended. Before Wyatt and Billy again take to the road, they have an innocent naked romp in a nearby stream with two of the commune girls.

The beautiful journey resumes. At the end of each day's run Wyatt and Billy camp at the roadside. We do not discover them buying or preparing their food, washing themselves or their clothes, or even actually building the fires over which they sit stoned. The inessentials of life have been eliminated to reveal life's essential joyous simplicty—obviously the two men supply each other with the kind of companionship in which marijuana is said to make its happiest effect: at any rate, they laugh together for no apparent reason. And if there is any doubt in the viewer's mind as to what it is that provides this nightly relaxation, it is nicely dispelled when the two men offer a cigarette to a drunk they have picked up who refuses it in terror—hasn't he, he asks, enough trouble already with the booze? Wyatt can reassure him: this anodyne has no devil in it as whiskey does.

The new member of what now becomes a trio of riders had joined them in the jail of his Southern town where he was sleeping off a binge. Riding into the town, Wyatt and Billy had playfully got entangled in a parade and been arrested. After a night in jail, the third young man, an ACLU lawyer, arranges for their release. Gentle, liberal, idealistic, he is the defeated son of the big man of the town, whose power is to be withstood only by drinking—the symbol of the son's remembrance of joy is a football helmet cherished since boyhood. Wearing his helmet, he hops a ride with his new friends: he is bound for a brothel in New Orleans. At a modest restaurant the trio attracts the attention of the sheriff and some cronies of his who mobilize a quick brutal hatred of the hippie outsiders; that night, as the three men sleep at the roadside, the sheriff and his people sneak up on them—they manage to kill only the local lawyer. Just as the sheriff stands for American xenophobia and violence, the lawyer represents, we must suppose, the soft liberal underbelly of American establishment. Well-meaning but misguided, he is first to succumb to a repressive social authority with which he had attempted to live and even deal, blind to its implacable enmity.

The pop music which functions as a kind of Greek chorus to the mounting doom of *Easy Rider* carries much of the emotion with which Wyatt and Billy receive the death of their new friend. They now undertake to complete his journey for him, and they go to the brothel in New Orleans, where they join up with two young prostitutes—but not sexually, only in comradeship. The four go together to the Mardi Gras, then continue the day in a cemetery where they get high on pot and liquor. By the time Wyatt distributes the LSD he has in his pocket, the girls are too intoxicated to care what they are taking. The inhabitable world vanishes from the screen: as in one of Dr. Leary's psychedelic celebrations, the film now is given over to describing the psychic states induced in Wyatt, Billy, and the two girls by the acid. We watch them writhe among the gravestones, suffering the apparently joyous agony of their self-willed release from the limitations of our reality-bound consciousness. When one of the girls takes off her clothes, no one has use for her naked body: with the help of drugs Wyatt and Billy have transcended more than our society, more even than their minds: their bodies. *Easy Rider* celebrates not only a pretechnological but also a presexual, or at least a pregenital, world.

But they have not transcended death. The acid trip over, the other journey across an America which once was, and presumably might still be, must once more begin. The two men get but a short distance beyond New Orleans, however, when they are overtaken on the deserted road and shot down, in coldest blood. Whether it is the same sheriff of their previous encounter or a counterpart who commits the murder, I am uncertain. But it cannot matter. What matters is that we have been shown vigilante America at work, out to destroy whatever loves freedom and is different from itself. The film ends in a bloody dawn, with Wyatt's and Billy's smashed bodies lying in the road. We understand that their murderers will go unapprehended.

This is, I think, a fair synopsis of *Easy Rider,* though not uncharged with my adverse feelings about the film. But it is necessary for me to make plain that although, while I was in the theater, I was aware of weighty reservations on the score of its moral content—they were provoked from the very start of the picture, by the sale of the heroin—I was also considerably seduced by it. It is not difficult for me to identify my seducer—ironically, it was America. I say ironically because, even apart from the fact that the point of the film is its attack upon America for failure to fulfill its promise to us, the America of *Easy Rider* is largely a pictorial illusion. The landscape it spreads out for us is mythic—I had almost said epic—in its lack of industrialization, of technology, even of population: I daresay there are still sections of the Southwest where one can travel big distances without seeing a billboard or a hamburger stand and where such farms as there are exist in isolation, but I doubt that one can travel from California almost all the way to New Orleans on main highways that are this totally bare of other humans and vehicles. And yet no other film that I can recall has so poignantly reminded me of the beautiful heritage we have in this country. It was the American land which seduced me in *Easy Rider*—and this would seem to suggest that I too, like the makers of the film, am caught in the dream of a country unscathed by modernity.

But the longing for an unravished land is obviously not a new emotion for Americans. It appears in our literature even before the existence of what can properly be described as a technological society, in the work of Cooper, Thoreau, Whitman, and of course Mark Twain—when Huck Finn lit out for the territory he too, even in his time, was trying to escape the restrictions of civilized modern life—and in our more recent literature it has played a decisive part in the imagination of Hemingway. For all of these men the unspoiled forests, prairies, mountains, and rivers of America make not only the setting for their quest of freedom but also the actual condition by means of which they discover their wholeness and worth as human beings. *Easy Rider* leans heavily upon the charm and authority of this literary tradition. But the unravished countryside which makes the landscape of its dream of the free life has, in fact, no integral relation to the film's representation of freedom—it is nothing *but* landscape. Its beauty is used, or misused, to validate the only freedom of which Fonda and Hopper have any genuine conception, that which is imputed to the drug experience. It is a first and basic dishonesty of *Easy Rider,* that is, that it proposes more than a kinship, actually an equivalence, or at least an interdependence, between the fulfillment which may be sought by moving beyond the frontiers of civilization and the gratifications which are sought in extending the frontiers of consciousness by the use of drugs.

But a dishonesty of this dimension requires other deceptions to sustain it. The search for a new frontier beyond which life will have retained its old innocence is, to be sure, recurrent in American literature, but we know it is not our sole American dream, nor ever has been: there has always gone along with our nostalgia for the fair and innocent land another dream, that of F. Scott Fitzgerald's Gatsby—the American dream of happiness through power and wealth. This was the conqueror's dream, and today we direct our sternest disapproval to those who submit themselves to it. Wyatt and Billy are so clearly presented to us as the very antithesis and negation of the predator's America that when at the end of *Easy Rider* they are destroyed by the forces of darkness, we are meant to feel that more than individual lives have been wiped out: virtue itself has been defeated.

Gatsby, we recall, tried to buy his transcendence over limiting social circumstance by bootlegging: Fitzgerald conceals from us no part of Gatsby's moral implication in this way of getting rich. Wyatt and Billy try to buy their transcendence over limiting social circumstance by trafficking in drugs, but they are made to bear no moral responsibility for *their* way of getting rich—unless we were perhaps to argue that their death at the end of the film is a punishment for wrong-doing, in which case *Easy Rider* would have to be accused of having vested its moral authority in cold-blooded murderers. The transaction in heroin is indeed embedded in moral obfuscation. We see the expensive white powder being given to the man in the Rolls-Royce, we never see to whom he gives it other than himself: we are never shown, say, the schoolchildren in Los Angeles who will become our newest statistics in heroin addiction and death. Certainly nothing in the film suggests that the money with which Wyatt and Billy undertake to escape this tainted world of ours is itself tainted—the sale of the heroin behind them, Wyatt and Billy represent the film's appeal on behalf of America's lost purity.

And just as the filthy business in which the heroes of *Easy Rider* make their wad is somehow disinfected by the presumed decency of their intentions in life, just so their recourse to heroin and LSD is somehow obscured by the innocent pleasure they have from marijuana. In general, the enlightened public now makes a distinction between marijuana and the other drugs which have come into wide use. In fact, the argument, not that all drugs should be legalized in order to take them out of the sphere of criminality, but that marijuana should be legal because it is harmless, rests on the belief that the use of marijuana is a quite separate activity from the use of "real" drugs. The evidence of *Easy Rider*, however, is against such a distinction. For Wyatt and Billy pot seems to be the basic daily fare which makes life supportable for them between their adventures with more potent medicines. We see the two men sniff heroin only once, at the start of the film; their practiced performance with it nevertheless makes us fairly sure that this is not an initial experience. Similarly, their composure after their bad acid trip suggests that this is not their first excursion in LSD. It is difficult to see how the young filmgoers who chiefly make up the audiences of *Easy Rider* can fail to conclude from the example of Wyatt and Billy that the sniffing of heroin and the taking of LSD are simply alternative to smoking pot, or, at least, that the taking of these more drastic drugs can be slipped in and out of at will, between joints, dreary medical injunction to the contrary notwithstanding.

Nor can we place more confidence in the social-economic import of *Easy Rider* than in its moral instruction. The film implies that spiritual freedom depends upon an escape from technology, and it gives us the happy rancher in example. In his barn a horse is being shod, and we are shown the wheel of a wagon—there is no farm machinery, there are no farmhands, and the rancher's sons are too young to help him. Apparently we are to believe that it requires only one man plus a horse and wagon to put a great tract of land under cultivation. We could perhaps accept a simplification of this sort as merely an aesthetic concentration, were it not for the extreme social and political disingenuousness of the film as a whole, including, as a prime instance, its assumption that one has only, like Wyatt or Billy, to be the target of evil forces within our corrupt society to be oneself wiped clean of all corruption. This curious assumption of course established itself in American liberal thought in the McCarthy period, when one had only to be the object of McCarthy's malignity to be warranted as forever blameless.

As in a traditional Western, *Easy Rider* divides the world into the good and the bad guys. But what gives *Easy Rider* its chic is its definition of good guys and bad in the sentimental terms which are at present being sanctified by left-wing thought: good guys want to be left in peace to live out their lives of natural freedom, bad guys want to impose their way of being upon others. In the revolution of the seventies the contending social forces are, of course, no longer labor and capital. They are the passively virtuous and the actively wicked. In *Easy Rider* the proletariat, with its auspicious place in history and its decisive role in determining the fate of mankind, is transformed into a pair of mindless cop-outs (not to say criminals) for whom there is neither past nor future, imagination, curiosity, desire. Symbols of what we are to suppose is the idealism and aspiration of this revolutionary day, Wyatt and Billy lack the energy to create anything, comment on anything, feel anything except the mute pleasure of each other's company.

But the muteness of *Easy Rider* not only accurately represents the anti-intellectualism of the contemporary revolution, it is also essential to the myth-making impulse of the film. By this I mean, simply, that were *Easy Rider* more verbal, more given to the exposition of its ideas, it would be more accessible to the skeptical intellect. For example, the pivotal point of the film, or at any rate what many viewers have taken to be its moral climax, depends upon our interpretation of a sudden statement by Wyatt—the statement consists of three words. Wyatt and Billy are once again about to hit the road after their acid trip, and Billy murmurs something about their having made it. To this Wyatt replies, "We blew it." This utterance might perhaps indicate that Wyatt thinks their journey has failed in its spiritual intention, or it might even suggest—which is not too different—that Wyatt has come to recognize his moral responsibility for the drug transaction. But nothing in the film supports such interpretations, and I am myself inclined to believe that the ambiguousness of the statement is a deviousness, and that it was formulated to allow the viewer to draw from it whatever moral conclusion would make him most comfortable. By staying with so few words and refusing to explicate Wyatt's summary assessment of his and Billy's quest, the authors of *Easy Rider* concur in an adverse moral judgment of the central characters of the film, if that is how we prefer it. But at the same time they protect the central figures of the film against adverse judgment so that they can be retained as examples of innocent victimization. And it is as examples of innocent victimization that Wyatt and Billy of course enter the pantheon of contemporary heroic dissent.

Here, then, are some of the lessons taught in this popular film, and an enticing brew of the fashionable, the false, and the pernicious they are. How are we to respond to such an offering? Surely not by legal censorship, which in America doesn't even raise questions of the control of moral and social ideas, only of what may be thought pornographic or obscene, and which in countries where it does treat such questions necessarily operates to suppress anything which challenges the assumptions of the official culture. But the rejection of censorship implies that we put our faith in moral and social intelligence either as exercised by the artists themselves or by those who receive their work.

It is a piety of our art-loving culture that between moral and social intelligence and artistic intelligence there is an inevitable congruence. *Easy Rider* is demonstration that this is not so. As an instance of the art of film-making, it is much to be praised: it is well played and well directed, imaginative, adroit, visually pleasing, and undoubtedly fulfills the intentions of its authors. But these positive qualities not only co-exist with grave deficiencies of moral and social intelligence; they give authority to the film's false view of the moral and social life. If *Easy Rider* were less attractive as a piece of film-making, we would not need to be concerned about its influence. It therefore rests with us who recieve the film to exercise the moral and social discrimination which the authors show themselves unable to exercise. In particular, this responsibility devolves, I think, upon those whose work it is to tell us how well the theater is fulfilling its high mission of instructing us in character and conscience: the critics.

It is my sense that more than any other group within the critical profession the film critics have the public's attention—for instance, less than a week after the warm critical welcome that was given the film *Z*, it was impossible to get a seat in the theater at eleven o'clock in the morning. I was out of the country when *Easy Rider* opened; but from the reviews I have since retrieved I have the impression, certainly not of general unqualified approval—only Penelope Gilliat of the *New Yorker* would seem to have given it that—but of a response in which any critical unease engendered by the film was always eventually, and effectually, buried in the reviewer's need to concur in what was taken to be its invaluable social message: it was as if Fonda and Hopper's observation of Middle America's hatred of anything different from itself and of the American capacity for mindless violence constituted an insight of such freshness and magnitude as to render paltry or carping any adverse judgment the critic might be moved to make on the film's validity as a document of American life. Except for Paul Schrader in the Los Angeles *Free Press,* who boldly ridiculed *Easy Rider* for its indulgence in stale left-wing ritualisms—and it is worth noting that with the publication of this review Mr. Schrader's connection with the paper was terminated—even critics who, like Richard Schickel in *Life*, spoke of the air of self-congratulation in which Wyatt and Billy have their being, or, like Joseph Morgenstern in *Newsweek*, mocked the sententiousness of the film, raised these objections in a context of appreciation.

And even Mr. Schrader went but half the course. Although he did indeed firmly denounce the nondimensional politics of *Easy Rider*, he mentioned not at all the means by which Wyatt and Billy financed their journey. The oversight, however, little distinguishes his reception of the film from that of the other reviewers. To be sure, Vincent Canby of the New York *Times* wrote: "After all, Wyatt and Billy, the heroin pushers, may be the same kind of casual murderers as the southern red necks." Stanley Kauffmann of the *New Republic* wrote: "In cold factual terms, Fonda and Hopper are pretty low types—experienced drug-peddlers, criminal vagabonds..." And Joseph Morgenstern, again in *Newsweek*, wrote: "Neither of these two riders...is conspicuously innocent. They've gotten the money for their odyssey by pushing dope." But these comments, which at least announce disapprobation of drug-trading, are curiously brief, unreverberant—they scarcely describe a rousing opposition to the film's own bland acceptance of drug-dealing—while the other reviews I have read fail to make even this small obeisance to the moral occasion. For Dan Wakefield, writing in this magazine, the drug in which Wyatt and Billy traffic is cocaine—he is positive in the identification. And extensively and eloquently outraged as Mr. Wakefield is by the bad treatment hippies receive at the hands of their fellow-citizens, he finds it possible to concentrate the whole of his judgment of Wyatt and Billy's drug transaction into a single sentence of narration: "The two hippies...make a highly profitable sale of some cocaine they score in Mexico to a sinister-looking connection in Los Angeles, and with the money stashed in the red-white-and-blue Stars-and-Stripes painted fuel tank of Wyatt's motorcycle, they take off east for New Orleans..." In fact, later in his piece Mr. Wakefield makes explicit his faith in the two central characters of *Easy Rider* as figures of virtue: "Why," he inquires, "the needless death and destruction of these fairly innocuous, generally pleasant, and harmless young men?" But it is left to Miss Gilliat of the *New Yorker* to bring the moral and social-political concerns of the film into most reassuring accord with each other. Of Wyatt and Billy she writes: "By smuggling dope across the frontier and selling it to a gum-chewing young capitalist disguised as a fellow-hippie, they make enough money to live life their own way." With a stroke of the pen, that is, Miss Gilliat certifies the heroes of *Easy Rider* as proper symbols of the lost freedom and decency of American life: they are genuine hippies rather than capitalists disguised as hippies, and they do not chew gum.

We are accustomed, of course, to the reluctance of our critics to submit to rigorous examination any political or social idea which offers itself as enlightened dissidence. It is indeed by its accessibility to whatever is opposed to established values or whatever may be regarded as innovative thought that criticism defends itself against the imputation of academicism and brings itself into the full current of strenuous contemporary life. Are we to conclude, then, from Mr. Wakefield's or Miss Gilliat's unperturbed acceptance of drug-dealing and from the self-effacing comments upon this enterprise on the part even of the critics who oppose it that drug use has made good its claim to radical-ideological status?

I do not think so. I think, rather, that what we are seeing in the less than satisfactory response of the critics to *Easy Rider* is their obedience to the modern injunction against moralizing about art. Quoting from Shaw, I said that the language in which Shaw described the function of the theater could only sound quaint to our contemporary ears. I meant that such outright moralizing puts us in mind of a culture in which there could be good firm working formulations of right and wrong and in which there were wise men, teachers, whose job it was to guide us through the few possible areas of doubt. Obviously, our sense of our own times is just the opposite of this. So extreme, in fact, is our awareness of the absence of such rules and of the lack of such persons, and of the consequent need for each one of us to improvise his own morality, that we have all but lost sight of the dynamics of culture. We forget that codes for the guidance of our moral lives are constantly being proposed for us by the culture.

In the fashioning of these codes the artists—especially, nowadays, artists in the popular media—have a primary role. But the role of the critics is far from negligible. It is the critics who are supposed to warn us not to be seduced by art and who are delegated to ask questions about the reliability and feasibility and worth of the codes which are being offered us. Theirs is always, if you will, a moralizing function. It is today, when they seem to be most moved to forget this responsibility, that they are perhaps most to be recalled to it.

15.4 Read the following selection which exemplifies theme development by various means.

Rock on the Rocks or Bubblegum, Anybody?

A year ago there were three AM radio stations in New York City that played only rock music. Now there is one. Four years ago dozens of discotheques and clubs featured rock music in New York. Now most of them are out of business.

Rock 'n' roll is dying. It is now going through the terminal symptoms that jazz went through in the '40s and early '50s. And it will die the same way jazz did—by growing up, by being transformed.

Jazz picked up most of its fans during its dance stage. Post-World-War-I flappers and Post-World-War-II beboppers crowded into ballrooms across the country to hear the new music and dance the night away to toe-tapping rhythms.

It's got a good beat. You can dance to it.

Rapport. For many years there was a close mutual appreciation between performer and audience. But as the art form matured, so did the musicians. They came to know much more about jazz than their audiences did. The fans knew nothing of the notation system, complex rhythms, time signatures. They just wanted to hear *Caravan* or *One O'Clock Jump.* A professional distance began to develop between artist and listener—some musicians looked on their audiences with contempt and took few pains to conceal it.

Distance from the general audience was reinforced by the appearance in the late '30s of a new type of fan. In the slang of the day these jazz followers were known as alligators. Like the

Irving Louis Horowitz, "Rock on the Rocks or Bubblegum, Anybody?" *Psychology Today,* 4 (January, 1971), 59-61, 83. By permission of the publisher.

groupies of the late '60s, they didn't dance—they stood in front of the bandstand all night and listened. Alligators understood. They knew the music. They knew the instruments and the soloists and they appreciated what they heard.

In this context many musicians came to define their own worth not in terms of the mass audience and the hit record, but in terms of peer approval. If the guys in the band and a few sophisticated fans appreciated what one was doing musically, then he was a success—and the rest of the audience be damned. Before they would play, the Modern Jazz Quartet and the Charlie Mingus Quartet often made outrageous demands for concert-hall levels of silence in their audiences. The jazz musician came to expect a nonemotional response to emotion. In some sense this is what the rock culture was originally in rebellion against.

The transition from get-up-and-dance music to sit-down-and-listen music took several years, but it was discernible in many later jazz bands—Cab Calloway's and Duke Ellington's, for example—and in the swing orchestras of Harry James and Benny Goodman.

Package. Finally, jazz moved from the dance floor to the concert hall. Norman Granz, the Bill Graham of his day, collected the biggest stars into one-nighter packages—Jazz at the Philharmonic—that toured the largest auditoriums in the country. These packaged performances stifled the creativity of many brilliant musicians, but there was big money in them. As Granz's malignant concerts spread through the land, jazz began to die.

The big bands acknowledged their mass audiences and, when pressed, they would play their familiar, danceable hits. But to maintain their self-esteem and professional integrity many artists sought other outlets. Small groups began to develop within the larger bands. The big band was for mass appeal—the small group was for displaying musical expertise and for building personal satisfaction. From Artie Shaw's orchestra came the Gramercy Five, and from Benny Goodman's big outfit came the Benny Goodman Trio. Instead of dancing, audiences were expected to sit and listen to Teddy Wilson's educated piano or to the cascading vibes of Lionel Hampton.

Thelonious Monk and Dizzy Gillespie achieved results similar to those of Bartok and Stravinsky—by innovating and creatively extending their traditions. The soloist became king, and Charlie Parker and, later, John Coltrane were canonized.

As the musicians grew older, so did their fans. Young, unsophisticated ears didn't know enough about the music to appreciate a good tenor-sax solo by Lester Young or Ben Webster. Artists became intraprofessional. Financial success ceased to be a criterion for musical esteem. The musicians who did reach mass audiences had by definition "sold out," and their sounds were disdained—they were "commercial" and "Tin-Pan Alley."

And then came rock 'n' roll.

It's got a good beat. You can dance to it.

The emphasis again was mass appeal. There were few intraprofessional standards, so an artist's worth was defined in the simplest, most obvious way—in terms of how many records he could sell. The focus was on the 45 r.p.m. single, and the Top 40 list was updated every week.

Every music reflects the society in which it flourished. In the Renaissance new needs for humanistic expression gave birth to tonal music which rejected the previous ecclesiastical doxology of the Medieval period. The ideals of freedom in the French Revolution gave rise to the chromatics and the gradual development from the sonata to the cyclical form of the Romantic Movement. Jazz itself, inherently an interracial music, represented a mixture of polyphonic African rhythms and modes with the tonal homophony of the European colonizers.

And rock music, a child of the technological age, reflects its parentage in every aspect. Each year amplifiers and preamplifiers get more sophisticated and more powerful, speaker systems get larger and louder, and new electronic gimmicks alter the sound or become part of it (feedback, cross-phasing, fuzz tones, wah-wah).

The contemporary recording process is so complex that a new group cannot make an album without sophisticated knowledge of electronics—mikeing, mixing, and mastering. Since *Sergeant Pepper,* the multi-track tape recorder has taken over. Voices and instruments are cut onto separate tracks so that the producer can make the piano louder than the bass on one chorus, or add echo to one voice but not another. Six months later, if he feels like it he can add a background of violins or cricket chirps.

Electronic experimentation has taken rock artists away from their roots—the song and the beat. To hear the Beatles as a group one must return to *Revolver,* vintage 1966.

Today's young take all the gadgetry for granted—they are not alienated by technological innovation, nor are they particularly impressed. Jazz musicians, on the other hand—especially followers of Gillespie and Monk—tend to resist technological innovation. Some, like Freddie Hubbard and Ornette Coleman, openly state their opposition to electronic music. They tend to think that any device not to be found in a 19th-century symphony orchestra is by definition not a musical instrument.

Hit. As rock has matured it has gone through many of the self-conscious changes that marked the rise and fall of jazz. In the first place musicians have changed their definition of success. The hit single is no longer necessary. A group can have a successful album without the support of a Top-40 single (for example, Jefferson Airplane, Jimi Hendrix, Country Joe and the Fish). And if an artist is respected by his fellow musicians, finds approval from a devoted circle of sophisticated fans, and is certified by a semiprofessional publication like *Rolling Stone,* he can maintain high self-esteem even while remaining relatively unknown (for example, Van Dyke Parks, Randy Newman, Captain Beefheart).

Some artists at their pinnacles—Bob Dylan, for example—have turned their backs on their audiences and retreated into seclusion. They may need to do this to preserve their sanity, but the effect is to increase the separation between artist and audience. The Beatles swore off personal appearances in 1966; Dylan retired to his Woodstock home after his motorcycle accident in 1966 and has made few public appearances since then; Elvis retreated from public appearances and holed up in his Tennessee mansion for nine years before his recent comeback at the International Hotel in Las Vegas.

Rock music has just entered the sit-and-listen stage. Even five years ago one could see the young dancing wildly to the omnipresent beat at San Francisco's Fillmore Auditorium. Now the fans don't dance—they sit, they concentrate, they get close to the stage so they can watch the guitarist move his fingers. They know rock music; they know the electric guitar; and they can tell immediately whether their favorite soloist is in peak improvisational form.

Super-groups. Just as the stars of yesterday's big bands sought professional recognition and creative opportunities by splitting off to form their own trios and quartets, the most talented musicians today look to each other for support in super-groups.

Many rock musicians have begun to look down on the mass audience. The leader of a top English group said after a recent U.S. tour that American audiences are indiscriminately appreciative—they applaud and yell for more, whether the performance is inspired or inept. This instills in the rock artist the same disrespect and contempt for the audience that the jazz musician felt when he finally gave in to a half-dozen requests for *Tico Tico*. Frank Zappa, on the first dissolution of the Mothers of Invention, complained that most audiences "wouldn't know music if it came up and bit 'em on the ass."

Rock is dying because it has matured and its fans have become self-selective. They sit intently and listen to complex guitar arrangements and improvisations. Eric Clapton, Mike Bloomfield, and Frank Zappa are being hailed as the greatest guitarists and rock musicians of our age. Their fans are devoted, musically sophisticated, and old. Young teen-agers find it very difficult to follow this improvisational music because they do not have background experience with rock. Their ears are not yet equipped to understand or appreciate complexity and innovation. Innovation is a break with tradition, and a 13-year-old has no tradition by which he can judge the improvisational forms being explored by many rock musicians.

Bubblegum. Young teen-agers don't like to sit and listen anyway. They want to move. And so they turn to the simpler, more danceable music that has come to be known as *bubblegum.*

It's got a good beat. You can dance to it.

To the disbelief and dismay of rock fans, bubblegum music has scored tremendous financial successes. *Sugar, Sugar* sold six million copies, making it the fifth largest-selling record in history. It is the Archies, Tommy Roe, and Bobby Sherman who get the golden records—not Traffic, not Leon Russell, and not Delaney and Bonnie.

Rock fans speak of bubblegum in a tone usually reserved for words like *excreta*. They look down on the 1910 Fruitgum Company with the same distaste that their parents reserved for Chuck Berry and Danny and the Juniors: *How can you listen to that garbage over and over? It's so simple, so repetitious, so childish.* Is this observation any more true of *Sugar, Sugar* than it was of *At the Hop?*

Different types of music appeal to different types of persons, yet there are always artists at the interface who want to reconcile the generations. Thus, in the mid-'50s white artists came out with cover versions of black rhythm-and-blues songs. In the early '60s rock songs became legitimate when they were set to the schmaltzy arrangements of Percy Faith, Ray Conniff, and the Hollyridge Strings. These albums catered to the older audience. The younger generation snickered as they would at a 50-year-old housewife who wore a miniskirt and headband. Staying young beyond one's chronology is a complex and often painful undertaking. As Jefferson Airplane explains: "One generation got old / One generation got soul."

Today there are fewer gap-bridging acts. This is partly because groups are providing their own nostalgic ties with older musical styles. A Mantovani version isn't needed any more—one can get lush, syrupy strings on the Beatles' last album, *Let It Be;* and on *Self Portrait,* Bob Dylan provides his own undercover versions of *Blue Moon* and *I Forgot More Than You'll Ever Know About Love.*

Voltage. In the search for new identity and innovation it was inevitable that rock would reiterate jazz. New bands don't feature just the electric guitar—trumpets, flutes, violins, and other traditional instruments are accepted in the contemporary rock band, as long as they are electric. Many recent bands (Blood, Sweat and Tears, Chicago, and Cold Blood, for example) are highly reminiscent in their instrumentation of such earlier groups as Miles Davis' Tentet in the late '40s. And the loud, brassy arrangements are direct descendants of Count Basie. A promising new group, Ten Wheel Drive, provides a mixture of Big Mama Thornton blues and a tenor sax reminiscent of Coltrane, all set to tight arrangements that remind one of The Jazz Messengers with Art Blakey and Horace Silver.

Other rock artists are reviving traditional jazz forms—on piano, Leon Russell sounds like Jelly Roll Morton, and Janis Joplin was certainly the best jazz singer since Ma Rainey and Bessie Smith.

With other artists—Miles Davis, Don Ellis, and Gary Burton, for example—the cross-fertilization between musical forms is so complete that classification becomes meaningless, or at least tedious.

Tracks. Other events in the evolution of jazz give hints of the future development of rock. For a brief period jazz found acceptance as background music in movies (*East of Eden, The Man with the Golden Arm*), and later served a similar function on action TV shows (Peter Gunn, Richard Diamond). Similarly, rock has recently found its way onto the sould tracks of dramatic movies (*Easy Rider, Zabriskie Point*), and we can expect that soon TV shows will feature rock 'n' roll theme music. After the extended stay of The Who at the Metropolitan Opera, anything can happen.

The musical statements that rock will make in its final years can only be guessed at. Innovation in style and song is essential in recent rock music—any group that fails to innovate does not attract a mass audience. No modern artist becomes popular on someone else's songs, unless he has arranged unique interpretations (e.g., Janis Joplin, Joe Cocker).

When any music reaches the sit-and-listen phase, it becomes a different music—jazz becomes *modern* jazz, rock becomes *hard* or *acid* rock. The music fails to pick up a new, young audience and it begins to die. Perhaps 20 years from now we will look back on Woodstock as the beginning of the end—similar to Benny Goodman's famous Paramount Theater and Carnegie Hall engagements of 1938. It may have marked the crystallization of the sit-and-listen phase, and therefore the imminent death of rock 'n' roll.

Perhaps 15 years from now there will be a bubblegum revival, the Archies will be likened to Bill Haley and the Comets, and Bobby Sherman will be called the musical genius of his time who broke away from tradition and forged the new music.

Sociological speculations are many and fascinating. But when some new musical form sweeps the mass audience out from under the aging bubblegum musicians, the young fans will have a clear and classic reason for liking the new music:

It's got a good beat. You can dance to it.